CAPITAL OF PAIN

CAPITAL OF PAIN
BY PAUL ELUARD

translated by

MARY ANN CAWS
PATRICIA TERRY
NANCY KLINE

with an introduction & essay by

MARY ANN CAWS

BOSTON, MASS.

CAPITAL OF PAIN
by Paul Eluard

Black Widow Press edition, September 2006

English translation © 2006 by Mary Ann Caws, Patricia Terry, and Nancy Kline
Introduction and essay on Eluard © 2006 Mary Ann Caws
Capitale de la Douleur © Editions Gallimard, Paris, 1926

cover photo: Paul Eluard © Stefano Bianchetti/CORBIS

Black Widow Press is an imprint of Commonwealth Books, Inc., Boston.
Joseph S. Phillips, Publisher.

All Black Widow Press books are printed on acid-free paper and put into sewn and glued
bindings

Black Widow Press
www.blackwidowpress.com

Book design by Nancy C. Hanger

Library of Congress Cataloging-in-Publication Data

Eluard, Paul, 1895-1952.
  [Capitale de la douleur. English]
  Capital of pain / by Paul Eluard ; translated by Mary Ann Caws, Patricia Terry,
    Nancy Kline, with an introduction & essay by Mary Ann Caws.
    p. cm.
  Translation of: Capitale de la douleur.
  ISBN-13: 978-0-9768449-6-9 (alk. paper)
  I. Caws, Mary Ann. II. Terry, Patricia Ann, 1929- III. Kline, Nancy. IV. Title.

PQ2609.L75C313 2006
841'.912--dc22

                                                                          2006022982

Prepress production by Windhaven Press (www.windhaven.com)
Printed by Thomson-Shore
Printed in the United States

10 9 8 7 6 5 4 3 2 1

CONTENTS

key to translators:

PT — Patricia Terry
MAC — Mary Ann Caws
NK — Nancy Kline

Introduction

Strangely or not, this particular collection of 1926 has made a lasting impression on more readers than one might suspect. Young Frenchmen between the wars carried it in their backpacks, other poets were dazzled, and even now, young and old, soldiers, poets, and just plain readers are no less so. It shows the freshness of early surrealism, as well as the despair of postwar trauma. Eluard was a member of the surrealist group, in fact a founder of it along with André Breton and Louis Aragon, and remained in the group from 1924 to 1936, when he, like Aragon, turned towards Communism instead. At a certain point, after the heady days of *La Révolution surréaliste*, the surrealists had put themselves at the service of the revolution and retitled their journal: *Le surréalisme au service de la révolution*, but the divergence between the Bretonian attitude and that of standard Communist cells, such as the one to which he was assigned, was too great and Surrealism as such went its way. That was not, in the long run, the way of Eluard, who in any case was always thought to be the most characteristic, and certainly was always the most celebrated poet among them.

Surrealist poetics have been widely discussed; and are illustrated in this volume by many aspects—the juxtaposition of clashing concepts or expressions, the apparent lack of any structure or coherent thought, the "automatic" procedure leading to the texts. In fact, this collection has been thought by many to be the key to grasping what surrealist texts are like. The reasons for the lasting success and

actual fame of *Capitale de la douleur* are of course diverse, but there
has been general agreement about its power. As to what exactly pro-
vokes the reaction in this wide-ranging and differently styled gathering of poems, readers will disagree. The poems may be light, even
silly, profound, ironic (see *"les petits justes"*) or quite beautiful; many
are enigmatic. My special favorites are the prose poems—on each
rereading, they seem to me to convey something else new, to turn
in yet another direction.

Some of the poems strike me as just plain bizarre—they are attractive to a surrealizing reader ... such as I am. Take, for example, *"Oeil
de sourd,"* the title of which already combines two senses: sight and
hearing (or rather, not hearing). Robert Wilson's *Deaf Man's Glance*, of
the same title, seems to have exercised the same peculiar power on its
audience.

"Do my portrait," it begins. ... The portrait, like most challenging
pictures, will change, it seems to fill up any empty space. But here's
the catch; you have to do this painting in total silence "Unless—if
it—only if—except"—and then, "I can't understand you." The reader
feels silence, distanced, unhearing and uncomprehending. *"Je ne vous
entends pas,"* says the pen, the verb *"entendre"* meaning both hearing
and understanding. That we have to choose exemplifies one of the
intriguing challenges of translation: it sends us straight back to the
question of translating the title of this collection: "pain" or by "sor-
row," the word *"douleur"* reading in both directions.

Capital of Pain is the way this volume has always been referred
to in English and so we kept it, noting the undercurrent of violence and physicality that there in fact is in this collection. Paul
Eluard had a genius for titles: within the present collection are
included poems from "Repetitions"—conveying, like so many other
of Eluard's chosen terms, an ambiguity fruitful for the imagination.
Rehearsals, it means, like a theatrical necessity, and also of course,
repetitions as in repeats. These poems are both. Another title reads:
"Mourir de ne pas mourir"—"Dying from not Dying" ... but mortal-
ity would certainly be hastened by this kind of spinning about,
like preciosity mixed with genuine feeling.

As for the widely-differing translations, each translator has, of course, an individual way of handling the texts chosen. When there is collaboration, some sort of miracle can often occur—as if there were two voices, or three in very rare cases—a kind of correspondence that a separate voice might not reach.

It has been a privilege to work on this volume, in its diversity and its singularity.

—Mary Ann Caws

RÉPÉTITIONS

REPETITIONS

Max Ernst

Dans un coin l'inceste agile
Tourne autour de la virginité d'une petite robe
Dans un coin le ciel délivré
Aux épines de l'orage laisse des boules blanches.

Dans un coin plus clair de tous les yeux
On attend les poissons d'angoisse.
Dans un coin la voiture de verdure de l'été
Immobile glorieuse et pour toujours.

A la lueur de la jeunesse
Des lampes allumées très tard.
La première montre ses seins que tuent des insectes rouges.

Max Ernst

In a corner agile incest
Circles the virginity of a little dress.
In a corner the sky turned over
To the spines of the storm leaves white balls behind.

In the brightest corner of every eye
We're expecting the fish of anguish.
In a corner the car of summer
Immobile glorious and forever.

In the light of youth
Lamps lit very late.
The first one shows its breasts that red insects are killing.

(MAC/PT)

Suite

Pour l'éclat du jour des bonheurs en l'air
Pour vivre aisément des goûts des couleurs
Pour se régaler des amours pour rire
Pour ouvrir les yeux au dernier instant

Elle a toutes les complaisances.

Sequence

For brilliant days of topsy-turvy joy
Easy living on the tastes of colors
Feasting on love for the fun of it
For opening her eyes at the last instant
She has a real soft spot.

(NK)

Manie

Après des années de sagesse
Pendant lesquelles le monde était aussi transparent qu'une aiguille
Roucouler s'agit-il d'autre chose?
Après avoir rivalisé rendu grâces et dilapidé le trésor
Plus d'une lèvre rouge avec un point rouge
Et plus d'une jambe blanche avec un pied blanc
Où nous croyons-nous donc?

Obsession

After years of behaving
With the world as transparent as a needle
Is there anything but cooing?
After having competed given thanks half-destroying the treasure
More than one red lip with a red dot
And more than one white leg with one white foot
Where do we think we are?

(MAC/PT)

L'invention

La droite laisse couler du sable.
Toutes les transformations sont possibles.

Loin, le soleil aiguise sur les pierres sa hâte d'en finir
La description du paysage importe peu,
Tout juste l'agréable durée des moissons.

Clair avec mes deux yeux,
Comme l'eau et le feu.

✳

Quel est le rôle de la racine?
Le désespoir a rompu tous ses liens
Et porte les mains à sa tête.
Un sept, un quatre, un deux, un un,
Cent femmes dans la rue
Que je ne verrai plus.

✳

L'art d'aimer, l'art libéral, l'art de bien mourir, l'art de penser, l'art
incohérent, l'art de fumer, l'art de jouir, l'art du moyen âge, l'art
décoratif, l'art de raisonner, l'art de bien raisonner, l'art poétique,
l'art mécanique, l'art érotique, l'art d'être grand-père, l'art de la
danse, l'art de voir, l'art d'agrément, l'art de caresser, l'art japonais,
l'art de jouer, l'art de manger, l'art de torturer.

✳

Je n'ai pourtant jamais trouvé ce que j'écris dans ce que
j'aime.

Invention

The right hand lets sand slip through.
All transformations are possible.

Far off, the sun sharpens on the stones its haste to finish.
Describing the landscape matters little,
Just the pleasing length of a harvest.

For my two eyes a brightness
Like water and fire.

❋

What is the role of the root?
Despair has severed all its links
Raising its hands to its head.
Seven, four, two, one,
In the street a hundred women
I won't see again.

❋

The art of love, liberal art, the art of dying well, the art of thinking, incoherent art, the art of smoking, the art of pleasure, medieval art, decorative art, the art of reasoning, the art of reasoning well, the art of poetry, mechanical art, erotic art, the art of being a grandfather, the art of dancing, the art of seeing, the art of charm, the art of the caress, Japanese art, the art of playing, the art of eating, the art of torturing.

❋

But I've never found what I write in what I love.

(MAC/PT)

Plus près de nous

Courir et courir délivrance
Et tout trouver tout ramasser
Délivrance et richesse
Courir si vite que le fil casse
Au bruit que fait un grand oiseau
Un drapeau toujours dépassé.

Closer to us

Running and running deliverance
And finding gathering up everything
Deliverance and wealth
Running so fast the thread breaks
At the sound of a great bird
You're always ahead of the flag.

(MAC)

Porte ouverte

La vie est bien aimable
Venez à moi, si je vais à vous c'est un jeu,
Les anges des bouquets dont les fleurs changent de couleur.

Open door

Life is very obliging.
Come to me, if I come to you it's a game,
The angels of bouquets with flowers of changeable colors.

(PT/MAC)

Suite

Dormir, la lune dans un œil et le soleil dans l'autre,
Un amour dans la bouche, un bel oiseau dans les cheveux,
Parée comme les champs, les bois, les routes et la mer,
Belle et parée comme le tour du monde.

Fuis à travers le paysage,
Parmi les branches de fumée et tous les fruits du vent,
Jambes de pierre aux bas de sable,
Prise à la taille, à tous les muscles de rivière,
Et le dernier souci sur un visage transformé.

Sequence

To sleep, with the moon in one eye and the sun in the other,
Love in your mouth, a lovely bird in your hair,
Adorned like the fields, the woods, the routes, the sea,
Around the whole world so lovely and adorned.

Flee across the landscape
Through branches of smoke and all the fruits of the wind,
Stone legs with sand stockings,
Held by the waist, all the river's muscles,
And the last concern on a face transformed.

(MAC/PT)

La parole

J'ai la beauté facile et c'est heureux.
Je glisse sur le toit des vents
Je glisse sur le toit des mers
Je suis devenue sentimentale
Je ne connais plus le conducteur
Je ne bouge plus soie sur les glaces
Je suis malade fleurs et cailloux
J'aime le plus chinois aux nues
J'aime la plus nue aux écarts d'oiseau
Je suis vieille mais ici je suis belle
Et l'ombre qui descend des fenêtres profondes
Épargne chaque soir le cœur noir de mes yeux.

The word

I am fortunate: mine is an easy beauty.
I slide over the roof of the winds,
I slide over the roof of the seas
I'm sentimental these days
I no longer know who's in charge
I no longer move silk over ice
I am ill, laughter and pebbles
I nakedly love whatever is most Chinese
I love what's most naked the darting of birds
I am old but here I'm beautiful
And the shadow coming down from the depths of the windows
Every evening spares the dark heart of my eyes.

(MAC/PT)

La rivière

La rivière que j'ai sous la langue,
L'eau qu'on n'imagine pas, mon petit bateau,
Et, les rideaux baissés, parlons.

The river

The river that flows under my tongue,
The water no one imagines, my little boat,
And, with the curtains drawn, let's talk.

(PT/MAC)

L'ombre aux soupirs

Sommeil léger, petite hélice,
Petite, tiède, cœur à l'air.
L'amour de prestidigitateur,
Ciel lourd des mains, éclairs des veines,

Courant dans la rue sans couleurs,
Pris dans sa traîne de pavés,
Il lâche le dernier oiseau
De son auréole d'hier—
Dans chaque puits, un seul serpent.

Autant rêver d'ouvrir les portes de la mer.

The sighing shadow

Light sleep, little propeller,
Little, warm, heart in the air,
Magician love,
The hand's heavy sky, the veins' lightning.

Running down the colorless street,
Caught in its paving stones,
He frees the last bird
From yesterday's halo—
In every well, one snake only.

Might as well dream you can open the gates of the sea.

(MAC/PT)

Nul

Ce qui se dit: J'ai traversé la rue pour ne plus être au soleil. Il fait trop chaud, même à l'ombre. Il y a la rue, quatre étages et ma fenêtre au soleil. Une casquette sur la tête, une casquette à la main, il vient me serrer la main. Voulez-vous ne pas crier comme ça, c'est de la folie!

✳

Des aveugles invisibles préparent les linges du sommeil. La nuit, la lune et leur cœur se poursuivent.

✳

« A son tour un cri: « l'empreinte, l'empreinte, je ne vois plus l'empreinte. A la fin, je ne puis plus compter sur vous! »

Nothing

Everyone says: I crossed the street to get out of the sun. It's too hot, even in the shade. There is the street, four floors and my window in the sun. A cap on his head, holding his cap, he comes to shake my hand. Would you please stop yelling like that, it's crazy!

*

Blind people you can't see lay out the sleeping clothes. The night, the moon and their hearts one after the other.

*

Then comes a cry: "It's gone! The mark is gone! It's gone! I can't see it any more. I can't count on you any more!"

(PT/MAC)

Poèmes

Le cœur sur l'arbre vous n'aviez qu'à le cueillir,
Sourire et rire, rire et douceur d'outre-sens.
Vaincu, vainqueur et lumineux, pur comme un ange,
Haut vers le ciel, avec les arbres.

Au loin, geint une belle qui voudrait lutter
Et qui ne peut, couchée au pied de la colline.
Et que le ciel soit misérable ou transparent
On ne peut la voir sans l'aimer.

Les jours comme des doigts repliant leurs phalanges.
Les fleurs sont desséchées, les graines sont perdues,
La canicule attend les grandes gelées blanches.

A l'œil du pauvre mort. Peindre des porcelaines.
Une musique, bras blancs tout nus.
Les vents et les oiseaux s'unissent—le ciel change.

Poems

You had only to gather the heart on the tree,
Smiles and laughter, laughter and the sweetness beyond senses.
Loser, luminous winner, pure as an angel,
High up toward the sky, with the trees.

In the distance groans a beauty who longs to struggle,
And who can't, lying there at the bottom of a hill,
And whether the sky is sullen or transparent
Whoever sees her must love her.

Days folding their fingers,
The flowers have all dried-up, their seeds are lost,
Dog-days are waiting for the great white frosts.

In a poor dead man's eye. To paint on porcelain.
Music, white naked arms,
The wind and the birds come together—the sky changes.

(PT/MAC)

Limite

Songe aux souffrances taillées sous des voiles fautifs
Aux petits amateurs de rivières tournantes
Où promenade pour noyade
Nous irons sans plaisir
Nous irons ramer
Dans le cou des eaux

Nous aurons un bateau.

Limit

Think of the sufferings carved under faulty sails
And the little ones who take pleasure in winding rivers
To drown in
We'll go cheerlessly
To row
In the bend of the water

We'll have a boat.

(MAC/PT)

Les moutons

Ferme les yeux visage noir
Ferme les jardins de la rue
L'intelligence et la hardiesse
L'ennui et la tranquillité
Ces tristes soirs à tout moment
Le verre et la porte vitrée
Confortable et sensible
Légère et l'arbre à fruits
L'arbre à fleurs l'arbre à fruits
Fuient.

Sheep

Close your eyes dark face
Close the gardens of the street
Intelligence and valor
Boredom and tranquility
In every moment these sad evenings
The glass and the glass door
Comfortable and feeling
Weightless and the fruit tree
The flower tree the fruit tree
Run away.

(MAC)

L'unique

Elle avait dans la tranquillité de son corps
Une petite boule de neige couleur d'œil
Elle avait sur les épaules
Une tache de silence une tache de rose
Couvercle de son auréole
Ses mains et des arcs souples et chanteurs
Brisaient la lumière

Elle chantait les minutes sans s'endormir.

The only one

She had in the tranquility of her body
A little snowball the color of an eye
She had on her shoulders
A spot of silence a spot of rose
A lid on her breast
Her hands and supple singing arches
shattered the light

She sang the moments without falling asleep.

(MAC/PT)

La vie

Sourire aux visiteurs
Qui sortent de leur cachette
Quand elle sort elle dort.

Chaque jour plus matinale
Chaque saison plus nue
Plus fraîche

Pour suivre ses regards
Elle se balance.

Life

A smile for the visitors
Who come out of their hiding places
When she goes out she sleeps.

Each day she gets up earlier
Each season more naked
Fresher.

To follow her gaze
She stands on one foot.

(PT/MAC)

Nul

Il pose un oiseau sur la table et ferme les volets. Il se coiffe,
ses cheveux dans ses mains sont plus doux qu'un oiseau.

*

Elle dit l'avenir. Et je suis chargé de le vérifier.

*

Le cœur meurtri, l'âme endolorie, les mains brisées, les cheveux
blancs, les prisonniers, l'eau tout entière est sur moi comme une
plaie à nu.

Nothing

He places a bird on the table and closes the shutters. He combs his hair, softer than feathers in his hands.

*

She tells the future. And it's up to me to verify it.

*

Bruised heart, soul in pain, hands shattered, hair gone white, prisoners, the water weighs on me like an open wound.

(MAC/PT)

Intérieur

Dans quelques secondes
Le peintre et son modèle
Prendront la fuite.

Plus de vertus
Ou moins de malheurs
J'aperçois une statue

Une sorte d'amande
Une médaille vernie
Pour le plus grand ennui.

Interior

In a few seconds
The painter and his model
Will flee.

More good things
Or fewer bad things
I notice a statue

A kind of almond
A varnished medal
More boredom still.

(MAC/PT)

A côté

La nuit plus longue et la route plus blanche.
Lampes je suis plus près de vous que la lumière.
Un papillon l'oiseau d'habitude
Roue brisée de ma fatigue
De bonne humeur place
Signal vide et signal
A l'éventail d'horloge.

On the side

The longest night and the whitest road.
Lamps I am closer to you than the light.
Butterfly the usual bird
Broken wheel of my fatigue
In a good mood places
Empty signal and signal
On the fan of a clock.

(PT/MAC)

A côté

Soleil tremblant
Signal vide et signai à l'éventail d'horloge
Aux caresses unies d'une main sur le ciel
Aux oiseaux entrouvrant le livre des aveugles
Et d'une aile après l'autre entre cette heure et l'autre
Dessinant l'horizon faisant tourner les ombres
Qui limitent le monde quand j'ai les yeux baissés.

On the side

Trembling sun
Empty signal and signal on the fan of a clock
One hand endlessly stroking the sky
At the moment when birds half open the book of the blind
And one wing after the other between this hour and the other
Sketching the horizon turning the shadows
Putting an end to the world when I lower my eyes.

(MAC/PT)

L'impatient

Si triste de ses faux calculs
Qu'il inscrit ses nombres à l'envers
Et s'endort.

Une femme plus belle
Et n'a jamais trouvé,
Cherché les idées roses des quinze ans à peine,
Ri sans le savoir, sans un compliment
Aux jeunesses du temps.

A la rencontre
De ce qui passait à côté
L'autre jour,

De la femme qui s'ennuyait,
Les mains à terre,
Sous un nuage.

La lampe s'allumait aux méfaits de l'orage
Aux beaux jours d'Août sans défaillances,
La caressante embrassait l'air, les joues de sa compagne,

Fermait les yeux
Et comme les feuilles le soir
Se perdait à l'horizon.

The impatient one

So sad about his false calculations
He writes his numbers backwards
And falls asleep.

A lovelier lady
And never found,
Looked for those rose-colored ideas of just fifteen,
Laughed without knowing it, paying no compliment
To the youth of his time.

Going to meet
What was going by to the side
The other day,

The woman feeling bored,
Hands on the ground,
Under a cloud.

The lamp lit up at the mischief of the storm
In the fine days of August without fail,
With one of her caresses she kissed the air, her companion's cheeks,

Closed her eyes
And like leaves in the evening
Faded out on the horizon.

(PT/MAC)

Sans musique

Les muets sont des menteurs, parle.
Je suis vraiment en colère de parler seul
Et ma parole
Éveille des erreurs

Mon petit cœur.

Without music

The silent ones are liars, speak.
I am really angry at speaking alone
And what I say
Awakens errors

Dear heart.

(PT/MAC)

Luire

Terre irréprochablement cultivée,
Miel d'aube, soleil en fleurs,
Coureur tenant encore par un fil au dormeur
(Nœud par intelligences)
Et le jetant sur son épaule:
« Il n'a jamais été plus neuf,
Il n'a jamais été si lourd. »
Usure, il sera plus léger,
Utile.
Clair soleil d'été avec:
Sa chaleur, sa douceur, sa tranquillité
Et, vite,
Les porteurs de fleurs en l'air touchent de la terre.

Glowing

Earth perfectly cultivated,
Honey of dawn, flowering sun,
Runner still holding the sleeper by a thread
(Knotted by complicities)
And throwing him over his shoulder:
"He's never been newer,
He's never been heavier."
With use he'd be lighter,
Useful.
Bright summer sun with
Its heat, sweetness, tranquility
And, hurry up,
The bearers of flowers in the air are touching the earth.

(MAC/PT)

La grande maison inhabitable

Au milieu d'une île étonnante
Que ses membres traversent
Elle vit d'un monde ébloui.

La chair que l'on montre aux curieux
Attend là comme les récoltes
La chute sur les rives.

En attendant pour voir plus loin
Les yeux plus grands ouverts sous le vent de ses mains
Elle imagine que l'horizon a pour elle dénoué sa ceinture.

The big uninhabitable house

In the middle of an astonishing island
That her limbs travel
She is nourished by a dazzled world.

The flesh one shows off to the curious
Waits there like harvests
To fall on the riverbanks.

Knowing she'll see further
Her eyes wider in the wind of her hands
She imagines the horizon has unbuckled its belt for her.

(NK)

La mort dans la conversation

Qui a votre visage?
La bonne et la mauvaise
La belle imaginable
Gymnastique à l'infini
Dépassant en mouvements
Les couleurs et les baisers
Les grands gestes la nuit.

Death in conversation

Who else has your face?
The good and the bad
Imaginable beauty
Infinite gymnastics
In mobility surpassing
Colors and kissing
Grand gestures in the night.

(NK)

Raison de plus

Les lumières en l'air,
L'air sur un tour moitié passé, moitié brillant,
Faites entrer les enfants,
Tous les saluts, tous les baisers, tous les remerciements.
Autour de la bouche
Son rire est toujours différent,
C'est un plaisir, c'est un désir, c'est un tourment,
C'est une folle, c'est la fleur, une créole qui passe.

La nudité, jamais la même.
Je suis bien laid.
Au temps des soins, des neiges, herbes en soins,
Neiges en foule,
Au temps en heures fixes,
Des souples satins des statues.
Le temple est devenu fontaine
Et la main remplace le cœur.

Il faut m'avoir connu à cette époque pour m'aimer,
Sûr du lendemain.

Still another reason

The shimmering air,
The air on a tower half destroyed but sparkling,
Have the children come in,
All the greetings, the kisses, the thanks.

Around her mouth
The laughter is always different,
It is pleasure, desire, torment,
A madwoman, a flower, a Creole passing by.

Her nakedness is never the same.
I myself am ugly.
In the era of solicitude, snows, solicitous grasses,
Crowded snows,
The era of fixed hours,
The statues' supple satins.
The temple has turned into a fountain
And the hand supplants the heart.

To love me, you'd have had to know me then,
certain of the future.

(NK)

Lesquels?

Pendant qu'il est facile
Et pendant qu'elle est gaie
Allons nous habiller et nous déshabiller.

Which?

As long as he is easy
As long as she is gay
Let's go put on our clothes—and take them off again.

(NK)

Rubans

L'alarme matérielle où, sans excuse, apparaît la douleur future.

C'est bien: presque insensible. C'est un signe de plus de dignité.

Aucun étonnement, une femme ou un gracieux enfant de toile fine et de paille, idées de grandeur,

Leurs yeux se sont levés plus tôt que le soleil.

*

Les sacrifiés font un geste qui ne dit rien parmi la dentelle de tous les autres gestes, imaginaires, à cinq ou six, vers le lieu de repos où il n'y a personne.

Constaté qu'ils se sont réfugiés dans les branches nues d'une politesse désespérée, d'une couronne taillée à coups de vent.

Prendre, cordes de la vie. Pouviez-vous prendre plus de libertés?

*

De petits instruments,

Et les mains qui pétrissent un ballon pour le faire éclater, pour que le sang de l'homme lui jaillisse au visage.

Et les ailes qui sont attachées comme la terre et la mer.

Ribbons

The real alarm in which, with no excuse, appears the pain to come.

Good: almost imperceptible. A sign of more dignity.

No suprise, a woman or a graceful child made of damask and straw, notions of grandeur,

Their eyes arose sooner than the sun.

The victims' gesture meaningless among the lace of all the other gestures, imaginary, five or six of them, towards the resting place—which is empty.

It's clear that they've taken refuge in the bare branches of a desperate politeness, a crown carved out by the wind.

Take hold, ropes of life. Are there any more liberties you could take?

Small tools,

And those hands squeezing a balloon to burst it, so that the man's blood splashes his face.

And the wings held together like the earth and the sea.

(PT/MAC)

L'ami

La photographie: un groupe.
Si le soleil passait,
Si tu bouges.

Fards. A l'intérieur, blanche et vernie,
Dans le tunnel.
« Au temps des étincelles
On débouchait la lumière. »

Postérité, mentalité des gens.
La bien belle peinture.
L'épreuve, s'entendre.
L'espoir des cantharides
Est un bien bel espoir.

Friend

The photograph: a group.
If the sun went in,
If you move.

Make-up. An interior, white and glossy,
Inside the tunnel.
"In the age of sparks
Light came pouring out."

Posterity, the mentality of people.
Such a pretty painting.
The proof, we suit each other.
The promise of Spanish fly
Is such a pretty one.

(NK)

Volontairement

Aveugle maladroit, ignorant et léger,
Aujourd'hui pour oublier,
Le mois prochain pour dessiner
Les coins de rue, les allées à perte de vue.
Je les imite pour m'étendre
Dans une nuit profonde et large de mon âge.

Voluntarily

A blindman, blundering, untutored, fickle,
Today in order to forget
Next month to sketch
Street corners, passageways as far as you can see.
I imitate them, stretching out
In this deep wide night of my age.

(NK)

A la minute

L'instrument
Comme tu le vois.
Espérons
Et
Espérons
Adieu
Ne t'avise pas
Que les yeux
Comme tu le vois
Le jour et la nuit ont bien réussi.
Je le regarde je le vois.

Punctual

The instrument
As you can see.
Let's hope
And
Let's hope
Goodbye
Take no notice
That eyes
As you can see
Day and night have succeeded.
I look and I see.

(NK)

Parfait

Un miracle de sable fin
Transperce les feuilles les fleurs
Eclôt dans les fruits
Et comble les ombres.

Tout est enfin divisé
Tout se déforme et se perd
Tout se brise et disparaît
La mort sans conséquences.

Enfin
La lumière n'a plus la nature
Ventilateur gourmand étoile de chaleur
Elle abandonne les couleurs
Elle abandonne son visage

Aveugle silencieuse
Elle est partout semblable et vide.

Perfect

A miracle of fine sand
Pierces leaves and flowers
Unfolds in fruits
And overflows the shadows.

Everything is finally divided
Everything lost, deformed
All breaks and disappears
Death without consequences.

Finally
Light is no longer itself
Greedy ventilator star of heat
It abandons colors
It abandons its face

A silent blindwoman
Everywhere the same and empty.

(NK)

Ronde

Sous un soleil ressort du paysage
Une femme s'emballe
Frise son ombre avec ses jambes
Et d'elle seule espère les espoirs les plus mystérieux

Je la trouve sans soupçons sans aucun doute amoureuse
Au lieu des chemins assemblés
De la lumière en un point diminuée
Et des mouvements impossibles
La grande porte de la face
Aux plans discutés adoptés
Aux émotions de pensée
Le voyage déguisé et l'arrivée de réconciliation

La grande porte de la face
La vue des pierres précieuses
Le jeu du plus faible en plus fort.

Round

Under a sun sprung from the landscape
A woman bolts
Her legs skim past her shadow
In herself alone she places the most mysterious of hopes

I find her credulous doubtless in love
At the locus of assembled paths
Of light attentuated to a point
And of impossible gestures
The great door of the face
With its plans discussed adopted
Emotions born of thought
The journey disguised and the coming of reconciliation

The great door of the face
The vision of precious gems
The shift of weakest into strongest.

(NK)

Ce n'est oas la poésie qui . . .

Avec des yeux pareils
Que tout est semblable
École de nu.
Tranquillement
Dans un visage délié
Nous avons pris des garanties
Un coup de main aux cheveux rapides
La bouche de voluptueux inférieur joue et tombe
Et nous lançons le menton qui tourne comme une toupie.

It isn't poetry that . . .

With eyes like that
How similar it all is
Naked school.
Calmly
In a slender face
We found assurances
A helping hand through rapid hair
The mouth of a low sensualist plays and falls
And we fling out the chin which spins like a top.

(NK)

Œil de sourd

Faites mon portrait.
Il se modifiera pour remplir tous les vides.
Faites mon portrait sans bruit, seul le silence
A moins que—s'il—sauf—excepté—
Je ne vous entends pas.

Il s'agit, il ne s'agit plus.
Je voudrais ressembler—
Fâcheuse coïncidence, entre autres grandes affaires.
Sans fatigue, têtes nouées
Aux mains de mon activité.

Deaf man's glance

Do my portrait.
It will change to fill all the spaces.
Do my portrait quietly, just silence
Unless ... if it ... only ... except ...
I can't hear you.

It's about, it was about.
I'd like to be like—
Regrettable coincidence, among other things that matter.
Tireless, heads joined
To the hands of what I'm doing.

(MAC/PT)

MOURIR DE NE PAS MOURIR

A André Breton

DYING OF NOT DYING

For André Breton

L'égalité des sexes

Tes yeux sont revenus d'un pays arbitraire
Où nul n'a jamais su ce que c'est qu'un regard
Ni connu la beauté des yeux, beauté des pierres,
Celle des gouttes d'eau, des perles en placards,

Des pierres nues et sans squelette, ô ma statue,
Le soleil aveuglant te tient lieu de miroir
Et s'il semble obéir aux puissances du soir
C'est que ta tête est close, ô statue abattue

Par mon amour et par mes ruses de sauvage.
Mon désir immobile est ton dernier soutien
Et je t'emporte sans bataille, ô mon image,
Rompue à ma faiblesse et prise dans mes liens.

Equality of the sexes

Your eyes have returned from an arbitrary country
Where the meaning of a glance has never been known,
Eyes have never been seen in all their beauty
Or pearls locked away, water drops, precious stones.

Naked jewels, O my statue, free of bone,
Instead of a mirror you have the blinding sun.
It seems to yield to powers of the evening
Because your head is closed, O my defeated one.

Thanks to my love and cruel strategies,
Immobile, my desire is all the help you've found,
No struggle when I seize you, O image that is mine,
Yielding to my weakness, and in my strong coils bound.

(PT)

Au cœur de mon amour

Un bel oiseau me montre la lumière
Elle est dans ses yeux, bien en vue.
Il chante sur une boule de gui
Au milieu du soleil.

*

Les yeux des animaux chanteurs
Et leurs chants de colère ou d'ennui
M'ont interdit de sortir de ce lit.
J'y passerai ma vie.

L'aube dans des pays sans grâce
Prend l'apparence de l'oubli.
Et qu'une femme émue s'endorme, à l'aube,
La tête la première, sa chute l'illumine.

Constellations,
Vous connaissez la forme de sa tête
Ici, tout s'obscurcit:
Le paysage se complète, sang aux joues,

Les masses diminuent et coulent dans mon cœur
Avec le sommeil.
Et qui donc veut me prendre le cœur?

*

Je n'ai jamais rêvé d'une si belle nuit.
Les femmes du jardin cherchent à m'embrasser—
Soutiens du ciel, les arbres immobiles
Embrassent bien l'ombre qui les soutient.

In the heart of my love

A beautiful bird shows me the light
In his eyes, easy to see.
Up on the mistletoe it's singing
In the middle of the sun.

❋

The eyes of singing animals
And their songs of boredom and rage
Forbid me to get out of bed.
I'm going to spend my life here.

Dawn in graceless countries
Looks like forgetfulness.
And if a woman deeply moved falls asleep, at dawn,
Headfirst, she's illuminated.

Constellations,
You know the shape of her head
Here, everything grows dark:
The landscape fills itself in, blushing,

The large forms get smaller and flow into my heart
With sleep.
And who intends to take away my heart?

❋

I never dreamed of so lovely a night.
The women of the garden are trying to embrace me—
Supports of the sky, the motionless trees
Completely embrace the shadow holding them up.

Une femme au cœur pâle
Met la nuit dans ses habits.
L'amour a découvert la nuit
Sur ses seins impalpables.

Comment prendre plaisir à tout?
Plutôt tout effacer.
L'homme de tous les mouvements,
De tous les sacrifices et de toutes les conquêtes
Dort. Il dort, il dort, il dort.
Il raye de ses soupirs la nuit minuscule, invisible.

Il n'a ni froid, ni chaud.
Son prisonnier s'est évadé—pour dormir.
Il n'est pas mort, il dort.

Quand il s'est endormi
Tout l'étonnait,
Il jouait avec ardeur,
Il regardait,
Il entendait.

Sa dernière parole:
« Si c'était à recommencer, je te rencontrerais sans te chercher. »
Il dort, il dort, il dort.
L'aube a eu beau lever la tête,
Il dort.

A woman whose heart is pale
Puts the night away in her clothes.
Love has discovered the night
On her impalpable breasts.

How can one enjoy everything?
Better to wipe it all out.
The man who moved in all directions,
Sacrified everything, conquered everything
Sleeps. He sleeps, sleeps, sleeps.
With his sighs he crosses out the tiny, invisible night.

He's neither cold, nor hot.
His prisoner has escaped—to sleep.
He isn't dead, but sleeping.

When he went to sleep
Everything astonished him,
He played ardently,
He looked,
He heard.

His last words:
"If I could start over, I'd meet you without trying."
He sleeps and sleeps.
In vain dawn raised its head,
He sleeps.

(MAC/PT)

Pour se prendre au piège

C'est un restaurant comme les autres. Faut-il croire que je ne ressemble à personne? Une grande femme, à côté de moi, bat des œufs avec ses doigts. Un voyageur pose ses vêtements sur une table et me tient tête. Il a tort, je ne connais aucun mystère, je ne sais même pas la signification du mot: mystère, je n'ai jamais rien cherché, rien trouvé, il a tort d'insister.

L'orage qui, par instants, sort de la brume me tourne les yeux et les épaules. L'espace a alors des portes et des fenêtres. Le voyageur me déclare que je ne suis plus le même. Plus le même! Je ramasse les débris de toutes mes merveilles. C'est la grande femme qui m'a dit que ce sont des débris de merveilles, ces débris. Je les jette aux ruisseaux vivaces et pleins d'oiseaux. La mer, la calme mer est entre eux comme le ciel dans la lumière. Les couleurs aussi, si l'on me parle des couleurs, je ne regarde plus. Parlez-moi des formes, j'ai grand besoin d'inquiétude.

Grande femme, parle-moi des formes, ou bien je m'endors et je mène la grande vie, les mains prises dans la tête et la tête dans la bouche, dans la bouche bien close, langage intérieur.

To be caught in the trap

It's a restaurant like any other. Does that mean that I don't look like anyone else? A tall woman beside me is beating eggs with her fingers. A traveler places his clothes on a table and accosts me. He's wrong, I don't know any mystery, I don't even know the meaning of the word: mystery, I have never looked for anything, never found anything, he's wrong to insist.

The storm which now and then comes out of the mist turns my eyes and shoulders. Then space has doors and windows. The traveler declares to me that I'm no longer the same. No longer the same! I gather up the debris from all my marvels. It's the tall woman who told me that this is the debris of marvels, this debris. I throw them in the streams so lively, so full of birds. The sea, the calm sea is between them like the sky in the light. The colors too, if you speak to me about colors, I am not looking any more. Speak to me of shapes, I have a real need of disquiet.

Tall woman, speak to me of shapes, or else I fall asleep and lead a remarkable life, my hands caught in my head and my head in my mouth, in my mouth well closed, an interior language.

(MAC)

L'amoureuse

Elle est debout sur mes paupières
Et ses cheveux sont dans les miens,
Elle a la forme de mes mains,
Elle a la couleur de mes yeux,
Elle s'engloutit dans mon ombre
Comme une pierre sur le ciel.

Elle a toujours les yeux ouverts
Et ne me laisse pas dormir.
Ses rêves en pleine lumière
Font s'évaporer les soleils,
Me font rire, pleurer et rire,
Parler sans avoir rien à dire.

A woman in love

She is standing on my eyelids
And her hair mingles with mine,
She has the shape of my hands,
She has the color of my eyes,
She dissolves into my shadow
Like a stone against the sky.

Her eyes are always open
And she doesn't let me sleep.
Her dreams in daylight
Cause the suns to drift away,
Make me laugh, weep and laugh,
Speak when I have nothing to say.

(PT/MAC)

Le sourd et l'aveugle

Gagnerons-nous la mer avec des cloches
Dans nos poches, avec le bruit de la mer
Dans la mer, ou bien serons-nous les porteurs
D'une eau plus pure et silencieuse?

L'eau se frottant les mains aiguise des couteaux.
Les guerriers ont trouvé leurs armes dans les flots
Et le bruit de leurs coups est semblable à celui
Des rochers défonçant dans la nuit les bateaux.

C'est la tempête et le tonnerre. Pourquoi pas le silence
Du déluge, car nous avons en nous tout l'espace rêvé
Pour le plus grand silence et nous respirerons
Comme le vent des mers terribles, comme le vent

Qui rampe lentement sur tous les horizons.

The deaf and the blind

Will we reach the sea if bells are shells
In our pockets, if the sea is crashing
In the sea, or will we rather be
The bearers of a purer, stiller water?

When water chafes its hands, it sharpens knives.
Warriors have found their weapons in the waves
And the clashing of their blows is like
Rocks wrecking ships at night.

It is thunder, it is tempest. Why not the silence
Of the flood? For in us is the space we've dreamed
To hold the deepest silence and we breathe
Like the wind on the tremendous seas, the wind

That slowly crawls over all the horizons.

(NK)

L'habitude

Toutes mes petites amies sont bossues:
Elles aiment leur mère.
Tous mes animaux sont obligatoires,
Ils ont des pieds de meuble
Et des mains de fenêtre.
Le vent se déforme,
Il lui faut un habit sur mesure,
Démesuré.
Voilà pourquoi
Je dis la vérité sans la dire.

Habits

All my girlfriends are hunchbacks:
They love their mothers.
All my animals are obligatory,
They have furniture feet
And window hands.
The wind is bent out of shape,
It needs a suit made to measure,
Measureless.
That's why
I tell the truth without telling it.

(PT/MAC)

Dans la danse

Petite table enfantine,
il y a des femmes dont les yeux sont comme des morceaux
    de sucre,
il y a des femmes graves comme les mouvements de l'amour
    qu'on ne surprend pas,
il y a des femmes au visage pâle,
d'autres comme le ciel à la veille du vent.
Petite table dorée des jours de fête,
il y a des femmes de bois vert et sombre
celles qui pleurent,
de bois sombre et vert:
celles qui rient.

Petite table trop basse ou trop haute.
il y a des femmes grasses
avec des ombres légères,
il y a des robes creuses,
des robes sèches,
des robes que l'on porte chez soi et que l'amour ne fait
    jamais sortir.
Petite table,
je n'aime pas les tables sur lesquelles je danse,
je ne m'en doutais pas.

Dancing

A table for children,
there are women whose eyes are like sugar cubes
there are women as serious as love unperceived,
there are women whose faces are pale,
others like the sky the night before the wind.
Little table gilded for holidays,
there are women of wood green and dark
the ones who weep,
of wood dark and green:
the ones who laugh.

Little table too low or too high.
there are fat women
with slender shadows,
there are hollow dresses,
dry dresses,
house dresses that love can't get out the door

Little table,
I don't like the tables on which I dance,
I didn't realize that.

(MAC/PT)

Le jeu de construction

A Raymond Roussel.

L'homme s'enfuit, le cheval tombe,
La porte ne peut pas s'ouvrir,
L'oiseau se tait, creusez sa tombe,
Le silence le fait mourir.

Un papillon sur une branche
Attend patiemment l'hiver,
Son cœur est lourd, la branche penche,
La branche se plie comme un ver.

Pourquoi pleurer la fleur séchée
Et pourquoi pleurer les lilas?
Pourquoi pleurer la rose d'ambre?

Pourquoi pleurer la pensée tendre?
Pourquoi chercher la fleur cachée
Si l'on n'a pas de récompense?

                —Mais pour ça, ça et ça.

Construction for fun

For Raymond Roussel

The man flees, the horse falls down,
Locked door without a key,
For the bird who makes no sound,
Death is the penalty.

A butterfly on a branch
Waits for autumn to end,
Heavy its heart, entranced,
Worm-like the branch will bend.

Why mourn the pressed flower?
And why for the lilac mourn?
Why mourn the amber rose?

Why mourn for the sweet pansy?
Why seek the hidden flower?
There's no reward for those.

But there's that, and that, and that!

(NK/PT)

Entre autres

A l'ombre des arbres
Comme au temps des miracles,

Au milieu des hommes
Comme la plus belle femme

Sans regrets, sans honte,
J'ai quitté le monde.

—Qu'avez-vous vu?

—Une femme jeune, grande et belle
En robe noire très décolletée.

Among others

In the trees' shade
As at the time of miracles,

In the middle of men
As though the loveliest of women,

Without regret, without shame,
I left the world.

—What did you see?

—A young woman, tall and beautiful,
In a black, very low-cut frock.

(NK)

Giorgio de Chirico

Un mur dénonce un autre mur
Et l'ombre me défend de mon ombre peureuse.
O tour de mon amour autour de mon amour,
Tous les murs filaient blanc autour de mon silence.

Toi, que défendais-tu? Ciel insensible et pur
Tremblant tu m'abritais. La lumière en relief
Sur le ciel qui n'est plus le miroir du soleil,
Les étoiles de jour parmi les feuilles vertes,

Le souvenir de ceux qui parlaient sans savoir,
Maîtres de ma faiblesse et je suis à leur place
Avec des yeux d'amour et des mains trop fidèles
Pour dépeupler un monde dont je suis absent.

Giorgio de Chirico

A wall denounces another wall
And the shadow protects me against my timid shadow.
O tower of my love turning round my love,
All the walls spinning white round my silence.

You, what were you protecting? Sky heartless and pure
Trembling you gave me shelter. Light standing out
Against the sky no more the mirror of the sun,
The daytime stars among the green of leaves,

The memory of those who spoke without knowing,
Masters of my weakness and I am in their place
With eyes of love and hands too faithful
Emptying a world where I am not.

(PT/MAC)

Bouche usée

Le rire tenait sa bouteille
A la bouche riait la mort
Dans tous les lits où l'on dort
Le ciel sous tous les corps sommeille

Un clair ruban vert à l'oreille
Trois boules une bague en or
         Elle porte sans effort
Une ombre aux lumières pareille

Petite étoile des vapeurs
Au soir des mers sans voyageurs
Des mers que le ciel cruel fouille

Délices portées à la main
Plus douce poussière à la fin
Les branches perdues sous la rouille.

Worn mouth

Laughter bottle in hand
At the mouth laughed death
Sleepers in all the beds
Beneath the bodies lies the sky

A clear green ribbon at her ear
A gold ring three spheres
        Easy for her to wear
A shadow looking like lights

For steamers a little star
Seas all alone in the twilight
Seas that the cruel sky scours

Hand-delivered delights
At the end softer dust
Branches lost beneath rust.

(NK/PT)

Dans le cylindre
des tribulations

Que le monde m'entraîne et j'aurai des souvenirs.

Trente filles au corps opaque, trente filles divinisées par l'imagination, s'approchent de l'homme qui repose dans la petite vallée de la folie.

L'homme en question joue avec ferveur. Il joue contre lui-même et gagne. Les trente filles en ont vite assez. Les caresses du jeu ne sont pas celles de l'amour et le spectacle n'en est pas aussi charmant, séduisant et agréable.

Je parle de trente filles au corps opaque et d'un joueur heureux. Il y a aussi, dans une ville de laine et de plumes, un oiseau sur le dos d'un mouton. Le mouton, dans les fables, mène l'oiseau en paradis.

Il y a aussi les siècles personnifiés, la grandeur des siècles présents, le vertige des années défendues et des fruits perdus.

Que les souvenirs m'entraînent et j'aurai des yeux ronds comme le monde.

In the cylinder
of tribulations

Sweep me away, world, and I'll have memories.

Thirty girls with opaque bodies, thirty girls who in the imagination are goddesses, draw near the man at rest in the little valley of lunacy.

The man in question is gambling fervently. He plays against himself and wins. The thirty girls quickly tire of this. Gambling's caresses are not those of love, and the sight isn't nearly as charming, seductive, and agreeable.

I'm talking about thirty girls with opaque bodies and one happy gambler. There is also, in a city of wool and feathers, a bird on the back of a sheep. In fables, the sheep leads the bird to paradise.

There are also personified centuries, the grandeur of present centuries, the dizziness of forbidden years and lost fruits.

Sweep me away, memories, and I'll have eyes as round as the world.

(NK)

Denise disait aux merveilles:

Le soir traînait des hirondelles. Les hiboux
Partageaient le soleil et pesaient sur la terre
Comme les pas jamais lassés d'un solitaire
Plus pâle que nature et dormant tout debout.

Le soir traînait des armes blanches sur nos têtes.
Le courage brûlait les femmes parmi nous,
Elles pleuraient, elles criaient comme des bêtes,
Les hommes inquiets s'étaient mis à genoux.

Le soir, un rien, une hirondelle qui dépasse,
Un peu de vent, les feuilles qui ne tombent plus,
Un beau détail, un sortilège sans vertus
Pour un regard qui n'a jamais compris l'espace.

Denise was saying to the wonders:

Evening was drawing swallows in its wake. The owls
Were taking turns in the sun and weighing on the earth
Like the untiring steps of a lonely man
Unnaturally pale and sleeping while he stood.

Evening was drawing white weapons over our heads.
Courage burned the women in our midst,
They were weeping, crying out like animals,
Troubled men had fallen to their knees.

Evening, a trivial thing, a swallow flying by
A little wind, the leaves no longer falling,
A fine detail, a magic stripped of power
For eyes without experience of space.

(MAC/PT)

La bénédiction

A l'aventure, en barque, au nord.
Dans la trompette des oiseaux
Les poissons dans leur élément.

L'homme qui creuse sa couronne
Allume un brasier dans la cloche,
Un beau brasier-nid-de-fourmis.

Et le guerrier bardé de fer
Que l'on fait rôtir à la broche
Apprend l'amour et la musique.

Benediction

Wandering, in a boat, up north.
In the trumpet of birds
Fish in their element.

The man who hollows his crown
Ignites a brazier in the bell,
A beautiful anthill-brazier.

And the warrior cased in steel
Who is roasted on a spit
Learns love and music.

(NK)

La malédiction

Un aigle, sur un rocher, contemple l'horizon béat. Un aigle défend le mouvement des sphères. Couleurs douces de la charité, tristesse, lueurs sur les arbres décharnés, lyre en étoile d'araignée, les hommes qui sous tous les cieux se ressemblent sont aussi bêtes sur la terre qu'au ciel. Et celui qui traîne un couteau dans les herbes hautes, dans les herbes de mes yeux, de mes cheveux et de mes rêves, celui qui porte dans ses bras tous les signes de l'ombre, est tombé, tacheté d'azur, sur les fleurs à quatre couleurs.

Malediction

An eagle upon a rock contemplates the blissful horizon. An eagle protects the motion of the spheres. Gentle colors of charity, sadness, gleams upon the bare trees, lyre with the shape of a spider star, the men who look alike under any heaven are as stupid on the earth as in the sky. And the one who drags a knife along the high grasses, in the grasses of my eyes, of my hair and my dreams, the one who bears in his arms all the signs of shadow, has fallen, splashed with azure, upon the four-colored flowers.

(MAC)

Silence de l'évangile

Nous dormons avec des anges rouges qui nous montrent le désert sans minuscules et sans les doux réveils désolés. Nous dormons. Une aile nous brise, évasion, nous avons des roues plus vieilles que les plumes envolées, perdues, pour explorer les cimetières de la lenteur, la seule luxure.

*

La bouteille que nous entourons des linges de nos blessures ne résiste à aucune envie. Prenons les cœurs, les cerveaux, les muscles de la rage, prenons les fleurs invisibles des blêmes jeunes filles et des enfants noués, prenons la main de la mémoire, fermons les yeux du souvenir, une théorie d'arbres délivrés par les voleurs nous frappe et nous divise, tous les morceaux sont bons. Qui les rassemblera: la terreur, la souffrance ou le dégoût?

*

Dormons, mes frères. Le chapitre inexplicable est devenu incompréhensible. Des géants passent en exhalant des plaintes terribles, des plaintes de géant, des plaintes comme l'aube veut en pousser, l'aube qui ne peut plus se plaindre, depuis le temps, mes frères, depuis le temps.

Gospel silence

We are sleeping with red angels who show us the desert without small letters and those sweet desolate awakenings. We are sleeping. A single wing destroys us, evasion, we have wheels older than the feathers flown away and lost, with which to explore the graveyards of slowness, the only lust.

The bottle we surround with the bandages of our wounds resists no longing. Let's take the hearts, the brains, the muscles of rage, let's take the invisible flowers of the pale girls and children joined together, let's take the hand of memory, let's close the eyes of recollection, a theory of trees delivered by the thieves strikes us and divides us, all the pieces are good. Which will gather them up: terror, suffering, or disgust?

Let us sleep, my brothers. The inexplicable chapter has become incomprehensible. Giants go by exhaling terrible laments, gigantic laments, laments of the kind the dawn wants to utter, the dawn now no longer able to complain, since then, my brothers, since then.

(MAC)

Sans rancune

Larmes des yeux, les malheurs des malheureux,
Malheurs sans intérêt et larmes sans couleurs.
Il ne demande rien, il n'est pas insensible,
Il est triste en prison et triste s'il est libre.

Il fait un triste temps, il fait une nuit noire
A ne pas mettre un aveugle dehors. Les forts
Sont assis, les faibles tiennent le pouvoir
Et le roi est debout près de la reine assise.

Sourires et soupirs, des injures pourrissent
Dans la bouche des muets et dans les yeux des lâches.
Ne prenez rien: ceci brûle, cela flambe!
Vos mains sont faites pour vos poches et vos fronts.

*

Une ombre...
Toute l'infortune du monde
Et mon amour dessus
Comme une bête nue.

No hard feelings

Tears in the eyes, the sorrows of the sorrowful,
Dull sorrows, dreary tears.
He asks for nothing, he isn't unfeeling,
He's sad in prison and sad if he's free.

The weather is sad, the night so black
You wouldn't put a blindman out. The strong
Are sitting, the weak hold power
And the king stands near the seated queen.

Smiles and sighs, insults grow rotten
In the mouths of mutes and the eyes of cowards.
Think nothing of it: this burns, that blazes!
Your hands fit in your pockets and against your brow.

*

A shadow...
All the bad luck in the world
And my love above it
Like a naked beast.

(NK)

Celle qui n'a pas la parole

Les feuilles de couleur dans les arbres nocturnes
Et la liane verte et bleue qui joint le ciel aux arbres,
Le vent à la grande figure
Les épargne. Avalanche, à travers sa tête transparente
La lumière, nuée d'insectes, vibre et meurt.

Miracle dévêtu, émiettement, rupture
Pour un seul être.

La plus belle inconnue
Agonise éternellement.

Étoiles de son cœur aux yeux de tout le monde.

She who doesn't speak

The leaves of color in the trees of night
And the blue-green vine joining the sky to the trees,
The great-bodied wind
Spares them. Avalanche, through its transparent head
The light, a swarm of insects, vibrates and dies out.

Miracle unclothed, crumbling, rupture
For a single being.

The loveliest unknown
Is always dying.

Stars of her heart in the eyes of everyone.

(MAC)

Nudité de la vérité

« Je le sais bien. »

Le désespoir n'a pas d'ailes,
L'amour non plus,
Pas de visage,
Ne parlent pas,
Je ne bouge pas,
Je ne les regarde pas,
Je ne leur parle pas
Mais je suis bien aussi vivant que mon amour et que
     mon désespoir.

The naked truth

"I know it perfectly well"

Despair has no wings,
Nor does love,
No face,
They don't speak,
I don't move,
I don't look at them,
I don't speak to them
But I'm just as much alive as my love and my despair.

(PT/MAC)

Perspective

Un millier de sauvages
S'apprêtent à combattre.
Ils ont des armes,
Ils ont leur cœur, grand cœur,
Et s'alignent avec lenteur
Devant un millier d'arbres verts
Qui, sans en avoir l'air,
Tiennent encore à leur feuillage.

Perspective

A thousand savages
Are fixing for a fight.
They carry weapons,
They have mighty courage
As they slowly form a line
To face a thousand green trees
Which, despite appearances,
Still value all their leaves.

(NK)

Ta foi

Suis-je autre chose que ta force?
Ta force dans tes bras,
Ta tête dans tes bras,
Ta force dans le ciel décomposé,
Ta tête lamentable,
Ta tête que je porte.
Tu ne joueras plus avec moi,
Héroïne perdue,
Ma force bouge dans tes bras.

Your faith

Could I be anything but your strength?
The strength in your arms,
Your head in your arms,
Your strength in the corroded sky,
Your stricken head,
The head I carry.
You will no longer play with me,
Lost heroine,
My strength flows in your arms.

(NK)

Mascha riait aux anges

L'heure qui tremble au fond du temps tout embrouillé

Un bel oiseau léger plus vif qu'une poussière
Traîne sur un miroir un cadavre sans tête
Des boules de soleil adoucissent ses ailes
Et le vent de son vol affole la lumière

Le meilleur a été découvert loin d'ici.

Masha was beaming

The hour trembling at the root of tangled time

A lovely feathery bird quicker than a speck of dust
Drags a headless corpse across a mirror
Spheres of sun soften its wings
And the wind of its flight maddens the light

The best was discovered far from here.

(NK)

LES PETITS JUSTES

JUST AND SMALL

I

Sur la maison du rire
Un oiseau rit dans ses ailes.
Le monde est si léger
Qu'il n'est plus à sa place
Et si gai
Qu'il ne lui manque rien.

I

On the house of laughter
A bird laughs in its wings.
The world is so light
That it's not where it used to be
And so gay
It has everything.

(MAC/PT)

II

Pourquoi suis-je si belle?
Parce que mon maître me lave.

II

Why am I so beautiful?
Because my master bathes me.

(MAC/PT)

III

Avec tes yeux je change comme avec les lunes
Et je suis tour à tour et de plomb et de plume,
Une eau mystérieuse et noire qui t'enserre
Ou bien dans tes cheveux ta légère victoire.

III

I change with your eyes as with the moons
And I am in turn lead or feather,
A dark and mysterious water holding you close
Or else in your hair a weightless victory.

(MAC/PT)

IV

Une couleur madame, une couleur monsieur,
Une aux seins, une aux cheveux,
La bouche des passions
Et si vous voyez rouge
La plus belle est à vos genoux.

IV

One color for Madame, one color for Monsieur,
One for the breast, one for the hair,
The mouth of passions
And if you're seeing red
The loveliest girl is at your knees.

(MAC/PT)

V

A faire rire la certaine,
Était-elle en pierre?
Elle s'effondra.

V

Make the sure one laugh,
Was she in stone?
She will melt.

(MAC/PT)

VI

Le monstre de la fuite hume même les plumes
De cet oiseau roussi par le feu du fusil.
Sa plainte vibre tout le long d'un mur de larmes
Et les ciseaux des yeux coupent la mélodie
Qui bourgeonnait déjà dans le cœur du chasseur.

VI

The monster of flight inhales even the feathers
Of this bird reddened by the firing of a gun.
Its lament resounds the length of a wall of tears
And the scissors of his eyes cut short the song
Already budding in the hunter's heart.

(MAC/PT)

VII

La nature s'est prise aux filets de ta vie.
L'arbre, ton ombre, montre sa chair nue: le ciel.
Il a la voix du sable et les gestes du vent.
Et tout ce que tu dis bouge derrière toi.

VII

Nature is caught in the nets of your life.
The tree, your shadow, shows its bare flesh: the sky.
Its voice is sand and its gestures wind.
And everything you say is moving behind you.

(MAC/PT)

VIII

Elle se refuse toujours à comprendre, à entendre,
Elle rit pour cacher sa terreur d'elle-même.
Elle a toujours marché sous les arches des nuits
Et partout où elle a passé
Elle a laissé
L'empreinte des choses brisées.

VIII

She is always refusing to understand, to listen,
She laughs to hide her terror of herself.
She always walked under the arches of nights
And everywhere she went
She left
The mark of broken things.

(MAC/PT)

IX

Sur ce ciel délabré, sur ces vitres d'eau douce,
Quel visage viendra, coquillage sonore,
Annoncer que la nuit de l'amour touche au jour,
Bouche ouverte liée à la bouche fermée.

IX

On this sky in ruins, on these panes of sweet water,
What face will come, sonorous ocean shell
To announce that the night of love is touching the day,
Open mouth linked to the mouth that's closed.

(MAC/PT)

X

Inconnue, elle était ma forme préférée,
Celle qui m'enlevait le souci d'être un homme,
Et je la vois et je la perds et je subis
Ma douleur, comme un peu de soleil dans l'eau froide.

X

Unknown, she was the form I preferred,
The one who freed me from the weight of being a man,
And I see her and I lose her and I bear
The pain like a little sunlight in cold water.

(MAC/PT)

XI

Les hommes qui changent et se ressemblent
Ont, au cours de leurs jours, toujours fermé les yeux
Pour dissiper la brume de dérision
Etc...

XI

Men who change and are like each other
Have, as long as they live, always closed their eyes
To dispel the mists of ridicule
Etc...

(MAC/PT)

NOUVEAUX POÈMES

à G.

NEW POEMS

To G.

Ne plus partager

Au soir de la folie, nu et clair,
L'espace entre les choses a la forme de mes paroles
La forme des paroles d'un inconnu,
D'un vagabond qui dénoue la ceinture de sa gorge
Et qui prend les échos au lasso.

Entre des arbres et des barrières,
Entre des murs et des mâchoires,
Entre ce grand oiseau tremblant
Et la colline qui l'accable,
·L'espace a la forme de mes regards.

Mes yeux sont inutiles,
Le règne de la poussière est fini,
La chevelure de la route a mis son manteau rigide,
Elle ne fuit plus, je ne bouge plus,
Tous les ponts sont coupés, le ciel n'y passera plus
Je peux bien n'y plus voir.
Le monde se détache de mon univers
Et, tout au sommet des batailles,
Quand la saison du sang se fane dans mon cerveau,
Je distingue le jour de cette clarté d'homme
Qui est la mienne,
Je distingue le vertige de la liberté,
La mort de l'ivresse,
Le sommeil du rêve,

O reflets sur moi-même! ô mes reflets sanglants!

To share no longer

In the evening of madness, bare and bright,
The space between things is shaped like my words
The shape of the words of an unknown man,
A vagabond who takes the belt from his throat
And, with his lasso, catches the echoes.

Between trees and barriers,
Between walls and jaws,
Between this great trembling bird
And the overwhelming hill,
Space has the shape of my glances.

My eyes are useless,
The reign of dust is over,
The hair of the road puts on its stiff cloak,
No longer fleeing, and I stop moving,
They've cut all the bridges, now the sky can't get through
I may not be able to see what's there
The world pulls away from my universe
And, at the very summit of the battles,
When the season of blood fades away in my brain,
I can tell the dawn from that human clarity
Which is mine,
I can tell vertigo from freedom,
Death from drunkenness,
Sleep from dream,

O reflections on myself! O the blood of my reflections!

(MAC/PT)

Absences

I

La plate volupté et le pauvre mystère
Que de n'être pas vu.

Je vous connais, couleur des arbres et des villes,
Entre nous est la transparence de coutume
Entre les regards éclatants.
Elle roule sur pierres
Comme l'eau se dandine.
D'un côté de mon cœur des vierges s'obscurcissent,
De l'autre la main douce est au flanc des collines.
La courbe de peu d'eau provoque cette chute,
Ce mélange de miroirs.
Lumières de précision, je ne cligne pas des yeux,
Je ne bouge pas,
Je parle
Et quand je dors
Ma gorge est une bague à l'enseigne de tulle.

Absences

I

The lackluster pleasure and drab mystery
Of not being seen.

I know you, colors of trees and cities,
Between us is the transparency of custom
In between sparkling glances.
It rolls over stones
Like rippling water.
On one side of my heart virgins are blurring,
On the other soft hands lie along the hillsides.
The curve of shallow water calls forth this falling,
This mixture of mirrors.
Precise lights, my eyes unblinking,
I do not move,
I speak
And when I sleep
My throat is a ring beneath the sign of tulle.

(NK)

Absences

II

Je sors au bras des ombres,
Je suis au bas des ombres,
Seul.

La pitié est plus haut et peut bien y rester,
La vertu se fait l'aumône de ses seins
Et la grâce s'est prise dans les filets de ses paupières.
Elle est plus belle que les figures des gradins,
Elle est plus dure,
Elle est en bas avec les pierres et les ombres.
Je l'ai rejointe.

C'est ici que la clarté livre sa dernière bataille.
Si je m'endors, c'est pour ne plus rêver.
Quelles seront alors les armes de mon triomphe?
Dans mes yeux grands ouverts le soleil fait les joints,
O jardin de mes yeux!
Tous les fruits sont ici pour figurer des fleurs,
Des fleurs dans la nuit.
Une fenêtre de feuillage
S'ouvre soudain dans son visage.
Où poserai-je mes lèvres, nature sans rivage?

Une femme est plus belle que le monde où je vis
Et je ferme les yeux.
Je sors au bras des ombres.
Je suis au bas des ombres
Et des ombres m'attendent.

Absences

II

I go out on the arm of the shadows,
I rest at the foot of the shadows,
Alone.

Pity is a step above, and may as well stay there,
Virtue offers her breasts to herself
And grace is caught in the nets of her eyelids.
She is lovelier than the shapes on the tiered steps,
She is harder,
She is below, amidst the stones and shadows,
I have found her again.

Here clarity fights its last battle.
If I go to sleep, it's so as not to dream again.
Then what will my triumphant weapons be?
I open my eyes wide in the assembling sun,
Oh garden of my eyes!
Here all the fruits embody flowers,
Flowers in the night.
A window of foliage
Opens suddenly in her face.
Where will I rest my lips, unbounded space?

A woman is more beautiful than the world where I exist
And I close my eyes.
I go out on the arm of the shadows,
I rest at the foot of the shadows,
And the shadows wait for me.

(NK)

Fin des circonstances

Un bouquet tout défait brûle les coqs des vagues
Et le plumage entier de la perdition
Rayonne dans la nuit et dans la mer du ciel.
Plus d'horizon, plus de ceinture,
Les naufragés, pour la première fois, font des gestes qui ne les
soutiennent pas. Tout se diffuse, rien ne s'imagine plus.

End of circumstances

A disheveled bouquet burns the cock-crests of combers
Peacocked feathers of downfall
Radiate in the night, in the ocean of the sky.
No more the horizon, no more the closed circle,
For the first time the shipwrecked make gestures that sink
them. Everything diffuses, nothing is ever imagined again.

(NK)

Baigneuse du clair au sombre

L'après-midi du même jour. Légère, tu bouges et, légers, le sable et la mer bougent.

Nous admirons l'ordre des choses, l'ordre des pierres, l'ordre des clartés, l'ordre des heures. Mais cette ombre qui disparaît et cet élément douloureux, qui disparaît.

Le soir, la noblesse est partie de ce ciel. Ici, tout se blottit dans un feu qui s'éteint.

Le soir. La mer n'a plus de lumière et, comme aux temps anciens, tu pourrais dormir dans la mer.

Bather from brightness to shadow

The afternoon of the same day. Lightly you move and, lightly the sand and the sea move.

We admire the order of things, the order of stones, the order of brightness, the order of hours. But this shadow which disappears and this painful element, which disappears.

In the evening, nobility has left this sky. Here, everything is swallowed up in a fire that dies out.

Evening. The sea has no more light and, as in former times, you could sleep in the sea.

(MAC)

Pablo Picasso

Les armes du sommeil ont creusé dans la nuit
Les sillons merveilleux qui séparent nos têtes.
A travers le diamant, toute médaille est fausse,
Sous le ciel éclatant, la terre est invisible.

Le visage du cœur a perdu ses couleurs
Et le soleil nous cherche et la neige est aveugle.
Si nous l'abandonnons, l'horizon a des ailes
Et nos regards au loin dissipent les erreurs.

Pablo Picasso

The weapons of sleep have dug into the night
Marvelous trenches keeping our heads apart.
Seen through the diamond, all medals are false,
The earth is invisible under the blazing sky.

The face of the heart has lost its colors
And the sun seeks us out and the snow is blind.
The horizon has wings, if we turn away,
And looking into the distance we dispel mistakes.

(PT/MAC)

Première du monde

A Pablo Picasso.

Captive de la plaine, agonisante folle,
La lumière sur toi se cache, vois le ciel:
Il a fermé les yeux pour s'en prendre à ton rêve,
Il a fermé ta robe pour briser tes chaînes.

Devant les roues toutes nouées
Un éventail rit aux éclats.
Dans les traîtres filets de l'herbe
Les routes perdent leur reflet.

Ne peux-tu donc prendre les vagues
Dont les barques sont les amandes
Dans ta paume chaude et câline
Ou dans les boucles de ta tête?

Ne peux-tu prendre les étoiles?
Écartelée, tu leur ressembles,
Dans leur nid de feu tu demeures
Et ton éclat s'en multiplie.

De l'aube bâillonnée un seul cri veut jaillir,
Un soleil tournoyant ruisselle sous l'écorce.
Il ira se fixer sur tes paupières closes.
O douce, quand tu dors, la nuit se mêle au jour.

164

World's first

To Pablo Picasso

Captive of the plains, dying and mad,
The light hides within you, see the sky:
Closing its eyes to catch on to your dream,
It's closed your dress to undo your chains.

    In front of the wheels tied together
    A fan bursts out laughing.
    In the treacherous nets of grass
    The roads forsake their glint.

    So can't you gather up the waves
    Its little almond hulls
    To hold them close in your warm palm
    Or the curls upon your head?

    Can't you gather up the stars?
    Stretched out you look like them,
    In their fiery nest you take shelter
    And your brilliance is multiplied.

    One cry wants to pierce the gagged dawn
    A revolving sun streams beneath the bark.
    It will light on your closed eyelids.
    O gentle one, when you sleep, night mingles with day.

(MAC)

[Sous la menace rouge]

Sous la menace rouge d'une épée, défaisant sa chevelure qui guide des baisers, qui montre à quel endroit le baiser se repose, elle rit. L'ennui, sur son épaule, s'est endormi. L'ennui ne s'ennuie qu'avec elle qui rit, la téméraire, et d'un rire insensé, d'un rire de fin du jour semant sous tous les ponts des soleils rouges, des lunes bleues, fleurs fanées d'un bouquet désenchanté. Elle est comme une grande voiture de blé et ses mains germent et nous tirent la langue. Les routes qu'elle traîne derrière elle sont ses animaux domestiques et ses pas majestueux leur ferment les yeux.

[Under the red threat]

Under the red threat of a sword, undoing her hair, which guides kisses and shows the spot where kisses rest, she is laughing. On her shoulder, ennui has dozed off. Ennui can only be itself with her, the rash one, who laughs as madly as day's end dispersing red suns beneath bridges, blue moons, faded flowers of a blasé bouquet. She is like a great wagon of wheat and her hands germinate and stick out their tongues. The roads that she tows in her wake are her pets and she closes their eyes with her sovereign steps.

(NK)

Cachée

Le jardinage est la passion, belle bête de jardinier. Sous les branches, sa tête semblait couverte de pattes légères d'oiseaux. A un fils qui voit dans les arbres.

Hidden

Gardening is passion, the gardener's beautiful beast. Under the branches his head seemed brushed by the feathery feet of birds. To a son watching in the trees.

(NK)

L'as de trèfle

Elle joue comme nul ne joue et je suis seul à la regarder. Ce sont ses yeux qui la ramènent dans mes songes. Presque immobile, à l'aventure.

Et cet autre qu'elle prend par les ailes de ses oreilles a gardé la forme de ses auréoles. Dans l'accolade de ses mains, une hirondelle aux cheveux plats se débat sans espoir. Elle est aveugle.

The ace of clubs

She plays like no one else and only I am looking at her. It's her eyes that bring her into my dreams. Almost motionless, at random.

And this other one she takes by the wings of his ears has kept the shape of his halos. In the accolade of her hands, a sleek swallow struggles hopelessly. It is blind.

(MAC/PT)

A la flamme des fouets

Ces beaux murs blancs d'apothéose
Me sont d'une grande utilité.
Tout au sérieux, celui qui ne paie pas les dégâts
Jongle avec ton trousseau, reine des lavandes.

Est-il libre? Sa gorge montre d'un doigt impérieux
Des corridors où glissent les sifflets de ses chevilles.
Son teint, de l'aube au soir, démode ses tatouages
Et l'asile de ses yeux a des portes sans nuages.

O régicide! ton corset appartient aux mignons
Et aux mignonnes de toutes sortes. Ta chair simple s'y
     développe,
Tu t'y pourlèches dans la pourpre, ô nouveau médiateur!
Par les fentes de ton sourire s'envole un animal hurleur

Qui ne jouit que dans les hauteurs.

In the flame of the lash

The apotheosis of fine white walls
Is very useful to me.
In all seriousness, the one not paying for the damage
Juggles with your keys, queen of lavenders.

Is he free? His throat points out, with an imperious finger
Corridors where his ankles are whistling by.
His skin, from dawn to dusk, his tattoos out of fashion
And the asylum of his eyes has cloudless doors.

O regicide! Your corset belongs to minions
And minionettes of every kind. There your simple flesh
        spreads out,
You climax in crimson, O new mediator!
Through the cracks of your smile a howling animal takes off

Whose lust is overly sated on the heights.

(MAC/PT)

A la flamme des fouets

Métal qui nuit, métal de jour, étoile au nid,
Pointe à frayeur, fruit en guenilles, amour rapace,
Porte-couteau, souillure vaine, lampe inondée,
Souhaits d'amour, fruits de dégoût, glaces prostituées.

Bien sûr, bonjour à mon visage!
La lumière y sonne plus clair un grand désir qu'un paysage.
Bien sûr, bonjour à vos harpons,
A vos cris, à vos bonds, à votre ventre qui se cache!

J'ai perdu, j'ai gagné, voyez sur quoi je suis monté.

In the flame of the lash

Metal that scars, metal of sun-sparks, nesting stars,
Pointed dread, fruit in shreds, rapacious love,
Knife-rest, foul defilement, flooded lamp,
Love's longings, dregs of disgust, whoring mirrors.

Oh sure—hello there, face!
Where light more clearly sounds desire than landscape!
Oh sure—hello to your harpoons,
Your cries, your leaps, and what you hide below!

I've lost, I've won, just look at what I've mounted.

(NK/PT)

Boire

Les bouches ont suivi le chemin sinueux
Du verre ardent, du verre d'astre
Et dans le puits d'une étincelle
Ont mangé le cœur du silence.

Plus un mélange n'est absurde—
C'est ici que l'on voit le créateur de mots
Celui qui se détruit dans les fils qu'il engendre
Et qui nomme l'oubli de tous les noms du monde.

Quand le fond du verre est désert,
Quand le fond du verre est fané
Les bouches frappent sur le verre
Comme sur un mort.

Drink

Mouths have followed the winding road
Of the burning glass, the starry glass
And in the well of a spark
Have eaten the heart of silence.

Mixture is no longer absurd—
It's here that you see the creator of words
Who self-destructs in the sons he engenders
And names the forgetting of all the world's names.

When the bottom of the glass is deserted
When the bottom of the glass fades out
Mouths knock on the glass
As on a deadman.

(NK)

André Masson

La cruauté se noue et la douceur agile se dénoue. L'amant des ailes prend des visages bien clos, les flammes de la terre s'évadent par les seins et le jasmin des mains s'ouvre sur une étoile.

Le ciel tout engourdi, le ciel qui se dévoue n'est plus sur nous. L'oubli, mieux que le soir, l'efface. Privée de sang et de reflets, la cadence des tempes et des colonnes subsiste.

Les lignes de la main, autant de branches dans le vent tourbillonnant. Rampe des mois d'hiver, jour pâle d'insomnie, mais aussi, dans les chambres les plus secrètes de l'ombre, la guirlande d'un corps autour de sa splendeur.

André Masson

Cruelty is knotted and agile sweetness is unknotted. The lover of wings takes on impenetrable faces, the flames of the earth escape through the breasts and the jasmine of hands opens upon a star.

The sky benumbed, the devoted sky is no longer upon us. Forgetfulness, better than the evening, wipes it out. Deprived of blood and reflections, the cadence of temples and columns remains.

The lines of the hand, so many branches in the whirring wind. The ramp of winter months, the pale day of insomnia, but also, in the most secret rooms of shadow, the garland of a body around its splendor.

(MAC)

Paul Klee

Sur la pente fatale, le voyageur profite
De la faveur du jour, verglas et sans cailloux,
Et les yeux bleus d'amour, découvre sa saison
Qui porte à tous les doigts de grands astres en bague.

Sur la plage la mer a laissé ses oreilles
Et le sable creusé la place d'un beau crime.
Le supplice est plus dur aux bourreaux qu'aux victimes
Les couteaux sont des signes et les balles des larmes.

Paul Klee

On the death-dealing slope, the traveler makes use
Of the favor of day, the slippery frost, no small stones,
And eyes blue with love he discovers his season
Beringed on all fingers with stars.

On the beach the sea has relinquished its ears
And the sand digs the spot for a beautiful crime.
Torture is harder for hangmen than victims
Bullets are tears and daggers are signs.

(NK)

Les Gertrude Hoffmann Girls

Gertrude, Dorothy, Mary, Claire, Alberta,
Charlotte, Dorothy, Ruth, Catherine, Emma,
Louise, Margaret, Ferral, Harriet, Sara,
Florence toute nue, Margaret, Toots, Thelma,

Belles-de-nuit, belles-de-feu, belles-de-pluie,
Le cœur tremblant, les mains cachées, les yeux au vent
Vous me montrez les mouvements de la lumière,
Vous échangez un regard clair pour un printemps,

Le tour de votre taille pour un tour de fleur,
L'audace et le danger pour votre chair sans ombre,
Vous échangez l'amour pour des frissons d'épées
Et le rire inconscient pour des promesses d'aube.

Vos danses sont le gouffre effrayant de mes songes
Et je tombe et ma chute éternise ma vie,
L'espace sous vos pieds est de plus en plus vaste,
Merveilles, vous dansez sur les sources du ciel.

The Gertrude Hoffmann Girls

Gertrude, Dorothy, Mary, Claire, Alberta,
Charlotte, Dorothy, Ruth, Catherine, Emma,
Louise, Margaret, Ferral, Harriet, Sara,
Florence stark naked, Margaret, Toots, Thelma,

Night beauties, fire beauties, rain beauties,
Heart trembling, hands hidden, eyes to the wind,
You show me light's gestures,
You trade a clear gaze for the springtime,

The curve of your waist for a flowery curve,
Defiance and risk for your unshadowed flesh,
You trade love for the thrill of shivering swords
An oblivious laugh for the promise of dawn.

Your dance is the frightful abyss of my dreams
And I fall and my falling makes my life eternal.
Under your feet space grows ever more vast,
Marvels, you dance at the springs of the sky.

(NK)

Paris pendant la guerre

Les bêtes qui descendent des faubourgs en feu,
Les oiseaux qui secouent leurs plumes meurtrières,
Les terribles ciels jaunes, les nuages tout nus
Ont, en toute saison, fêté cette statue.

Elle est belle, statue vivante de l'amour.
O neige de midi, soleil sur tous les ventres,
O flammes du sommeil sur un visage d'ange
Et sur toutes les nuits et sur tous les visages.

Silence. Le silence éclatant de ses rêves
Caresse l'horizon. Ses rêves sont les nôtres
Et les mains de désir qu'elle impose à son glaive
Enivrent d'ouragans le monde délivré.

Paris in wartime

Animals coming down from the suburbs aflame,
Birds agitating murderous feathers,
A terrible yellow sky, clouds that are bare,
To that one statue, all year long, bring praise.

Beautiful is the living statue of love,
O noontime snow, bellies warm in the sun,
O flames of sleep on an angelic face,
On all of the nights, on each and every face.

Silence. Resounding silence of her dreams
Caresses the horizon. Her dreams are ours.
From the blade of her sword, forced to desire's hands,
Tempests intoxicate the world set free.

(PT)

[L'icône aérée qui se conjugue]

L'icône aérée qui se conjugue isolément peut faire une place décisive à la plus fausse des couronnes ovales, crâne de Dieu, polluée par la terreur. L'os gâté par l'eau, ironie à flots irrités qui domine de ses yeux froids comme l'aiguille sur la machine des bonnes mères la tranche du globe que nous n'avons pas choisie.

Doux constructeurs las des églises, doux constructeurs aux tempes de briques rosés, aux yeux grillés d'espoir, la tâche que vous deviez faire est pour toujours inachevée. Maisons plus fragiles que les paupières d'un mourant, allaient-ils s'y employer à qui perd gagne? Boîtes de perles avec, aux vitres, des visages multicolores qui ne se doutent jamais de la pluie ou du beau temps, du soleil d'ivoire ou de la lune tour à tour de soufre et d'acajou, grands animaux immobiles dans les veines du temps, l'aube de midi, l'aube de minuit, l'aube qui n'a jamais rien commencé ni rien fini, cette cloche qui partout et sans cesse sonne le milieu, le cœur de toute chose, ne vous gênera pas. Grandes couvertures de plomb sur des chevelures lisses et odorantes, grand amour transparent sur des corps printaniers, délicats esclaves des prisonniers, vos gestes sont les échelles de votre force, vos larmes ont terni l'insouciance de vos maîtres impuissante et désormais vous pouvez rire effrontément rire, bouquet d'épées, rire, vent de poussière, rire comme arcs-en-ciel tombés de leur balance, comme un poisson géant qui tourne sur lui-même. La liberté a quitté votre corps.

[The airborne icon which conjugates itself]

The airborne icon which conjugates itself in isolation can make a decisive place for the most false of oval crowns, skull of God, polluted by terror. The bone spoiled by the water, irritated floods of irony dominating with its cold eyes like the needle on the machine of good mothers the slice of the globe that we didn't choose.

Gentle builders tired of churches, gentle builders with rose-brick temples, eyes grilled with hope, the task you were to do is forever unfinished. Houses more fragile than a dying man's eyelids, were they about to play the game of who loses wins? Boxes of pearls with, at the windowpanes, multicolored faces never suspecting rain or good weather, an ivory sun or a moon either sulfur or mahogany, great motionless animals in the veins of time, the dawn of noon, the dawn of midnight, the dawn which never began or ended anything, this bell that everywhere ceaselessly rings the middle, the heart of everything, it won't bother you. Great blankets of lead on smooth fragrant hair, great transparent love upon springtime bodies, delicate slaves of prisoners, your gestures are the ladders of your strength, your tears have dimmed the uncaring of your impotent masters, and from now on, you can laugh with effrontery, laughter, bouquet of swords, laughter, wind of dust, laughter like rainbows fallen from their scales, like a giant fish turning on itself. Freedom has left your body.

(MAC)

[Le diamant qu'il ne t'a pas donné]

Le diamant qu'il ne t'a pas donné c'est parce qu'il l'a eu à la fin de sa vie, il n'en connaissait plus la musique, il ne pouvait plus le lancer en l'air, il avait perdu l'illusion du soleil, il ne voyait plus la pierre de ta nudité, chaton de cette bague tournée vers toi.

De l'arabesque qui fermait les lieux d'ivresse, la ronce douce, squelette de ton pouce et tous ces signes précurseurs de l'incendie animal qui dévorera en un clin de retour de flamme ta grâce de la Sainte-Claire.

Dans les lieux d'ivresse, la bourrasque de palmes et de vin noir fait rage. Les figures dentelées du jugement d'hier conservent aux journées leurs heures entrouvertes. Es-tu sûre, héroïne aux sens de phare, d'avoir vaincu la miséricorde et l'ombre, ces deux sœurs lavandières, prenons-les à la gorge, elles ne sont pas jolies et pour ce que nous voulons en faire, le monde se détachera bien assez vite de leur crinière peignant l'encens sur le bord des fontaines.

[The diamond he didn't give you]

The diamond he didn't give you, it's because he had it at the end of his life, no longer knew its music, could no longer toss it into the air, he had lost the illusion of the sun, he no longer saw the stone of your nakedness, in which is set this ring turned in your direction.

From the arabesque surrounding the places of intoxication, the sweet root, the skeleton of your thumb and all these signs precursors of the animal fire that will devour in a turning of its flame the grace of Santa Clara which is yours.

In the places of intoxication, the whirlwind of palms and black wine rages. The jagged figures of yesterday's judgment keep for the days their half-open hours. Are you sure, heroine with lighthouse senses, of having vanquished compassion and shadow, those two washerwoman sisters, let's seize them by the throat, they are not pretty and for what we want to do with them, the world will detach itself rather quickly from their manes of hair painting incense on the edge of the fountains.

(MAC/PT)

[Sur la prairie]

L'hiver sur la prairie apporte des souris.
J'ai rencontré la jeunesse.
Toute nue aux plis de satin bleu,
Elle riait du présent, mon bel esclave.

Les regards dans les rênes du coursier,
Délivrant le bercement des palmes de mon sang,
Je découvre soudain le raisin des façades couchées sur le soleil,
Fourrure du drapeau des détroits insensibles.

La consolation graine perdue,
Le remords pluie fondue,
La douleur bouche en cœur
Et mes larges mains luttent.

La tête antique du modèle
Rougit devant ma modestie.
Je l'ignore, je la bouscule.
O! lettre aux timbres incendiaires
Qu'un bel espion n'envoya pas!
Il glissa une hache de pierre
Dans la chemise de ses filles,
De ses filles tristes et paresseuses.

A terre, à terre tout ce qui nage!
A terre, à terre tout ce qui vole!
J'ai besoin des poissons pour porter ma couronne
Autour de mon front,

J'ai besoin des oiseaux pour parler à la foule.

[On the meadow]

Winter ice on the meadow brings mice.
I have encountered youth.
Naked against folds of blue satin,
She laughed at the present, my beautiful slave.

Gazes in the charger's reins
Releasing the rocking of palms in my blood,
I discover abruptly the grapes of facades that have set on the sun,
Fur of the flag of unfeeling straits.

Consolation wasted grain,
Contrition melted rain,
In pain my mouth is in my heart
My wide hands are at war.

The model's ancient head
Blushes before my modesty.
I ignore it, I knock it over.
Oh! letter bearing incendiary stamps
Never posted by a handsome spy!
He slid an ax of stone
Inside his daughters' shirts,
His lazy sorrowful daughters.

To earth, to earth, everything that swims!
To earth, to earth, everything that flies!
I need fish to support my crown
Around my brow,

I need birds to address the crowd.

(NK)

[Grandes conspiratrices]

Grandes conspiratrices, routes sans destinée, croisant l'x de mes pas hésitants, nattes gonflées de pierres ou de neige, puits légers dans l'espace, rayons de la roue des voyages, routes de brises et d'orages, routes viriles dans les champs humides, routes féminines dans les villes, ficelles d'une toupie folle, l'homme, à vous fréquenter, perd son chemin et cette vertu qui le condamne aux buts. Il dénoue sa présence, il abdique son image et rêve que les étoiles vont se guider sur lui.

[Great conspirators]

Great conspirators, roads without a destiny, crossing the x of my hesitant steps, braids swollen with stones or snow, wells weightless in space, spokes of the wheel of voyages, roads of light winds and storms, virile roads in the damp fields, feminine roads in the towns, threads of a madly spinning top, whoever frequents you loses his way and this quality that condemns him to certain goals. He forsakes his presence, he abdicates his image, and dreams that the stars are going to take him as a guide.

(MAC)

Leurs yeux toujours purs

Jours de lenteur, jours de pluie,
Jours de miroirs brisés et d'aiguilles perdues,
Jours de paupières closes à l'horizon des mers,
D'heures toutes semblables, jours de captivité,

Mon esprit qui brillait encore sur les feuilles
Et les rieurs, mon esprit est nu comme l'amour,
L'aurore qu'il oublie lui fait baisser la tête
Et contempler son corps obéissant et vain.

Pourtant, j'ai vu les plus beaux yeux du monde,
Dieux d'argent qui tenaient des saphirs dans leurs mains,
De véritables dieux, des oiseaux dans la terre
Et dans l'eau, je les ai vus.

Leurs ailes sont les miennes, rien n'existe
Que leur vol qui secoue ma misère.
Leur vol d'étoile et de lumière
Leur vol de terre, leur vol de pierre
Sur les flots de leurs ailes,

Ma pensée soutenue par la vie et la mort.

Their eyes always pure

Days of slowness, days of rains
Days of broken mirrors and misplaced needles,
Days of eyelids shut against the line of the sea,
Of hours all alike, days of captivity,

My spirit still shining on the leaves
And on the flowers, my spirit is as naked as love,
The dawn, forgotten, forces it to look down
At its useless, obedient body.

And yet, I have seen the most beautiful eyes in the world,
Gods of silver, sapphires in their hands
True gods, birds of the earth,
Water-birds, I have seen them.

Their wings are mine, nothing
Shakes off my misery but their flight,
Flight of star and of light
Flight of earth, flight of stone
Afloat on their wings,

Life and death holding my thought aloft.

(NK)

Max Ernst

Dévoré par les plumes et soumis à la mer,
Il a laissé passer son ombre dans le vol
Des oiseaux de la liberté.
Il a laissé
La rampe à ceux qui tombent sous la pluie,
Il a laissé leur toit à tous ceux qui se vérifient.

Son corps était en ordre,
Le corps des autres est venu disperser
Cette ordonnance qu'il tenait
De la première empreinte de son sang sur terre.

Ses yeux sont dans un mur
Et son visage est leur lourde parure.
Un mensonge de plus du jour,
Une nuit de plus, il n'y a plus d'aveugles.

Max Ernst

Devoured by feathers and subject to the sea,
He has let his shadow pass by in the flight
Of the birds of freedom.
He has left
The ramp to those falling under the rain,
He has left their roof to all those proving themselves.

His body was in order,
The body of others came to disperse
This prescription he kept
From the first imprint of his blood on the earth.

His eyes are in a wall
And his face is their heavy ornament.
One more lie of the day
One more night, no more blind men.

(MAC)

Une

Je suis tombé de ma fureur, la fatigue me défigure, mais je vous aperçois encore, femmes bruyantes, étoiles muettes, je vous apercevrai toujours, folie.

Et toi, le sang des astres coule en toi, leur lumière te soutient. Sur les fleurs, tu te dresses avec les fleurs, sur les pierres avec les pierres.

Blanche éteinte des souvenirs, étalée, étoilée, rayonnante de tes larmes qui fuient. Je suis perdu.

One

I have fallen from my fury, fatigue disfigures me, but I still see you, noisy women, mute stars, I shall see you always, madness.

And you, the blood of stars runs through you, their light sustains you. On the flowers, you rise up with the flowers, on the stones with the stones.

Exhausted whiteness of memories, spread out, starred, radiant with your tears that run by. I am lost.

(MAC)

Le plus jeune

Au plafond de la libellule
Un enfant fou s'est pendu,
Fixement regarde l'herbe,
Confiant lève les yeux:
Le brouillard léger se lèche comme un chat
Qui se dépouille de ses rêves.
L'enfant sait que le monde commence à peine:
Tout est transparent,
C'est la lune qui est au centre de la terre,
C'est la verdure qui couvre le ciel
Et c'est dans les yeux de l'enfant,
Dans ses yeux sombres et profonds
Comme les nuits blanches
Que naît la lumière.

The youngest

Around the ceiling of the dragonfly
A mad child has draped himself,
Unblinking gazes at the grass,
Confident lifts up his eyes:
The light fog licks itself like a cat
That is sloughing off its dreams.
The child knows the world has just barely begun:
Everything's transparent,
The center of earth is the moon,
Greenery arches over the sky,
It's the eyes of the child,
His eyes dark and deep
As insomniac nights
That give birth to the light.

(NK)

Au hasard

Au hasard une épopée mais bien finie maintenant,
Tous les actes sont prisonniers
D'esclaves à barbe d'ancêtre
Et les paroles coutumières
Ne valent que dans leur mémoire.

Au hasard tout ce qui brûle, tout ce qui ronge,
Tout ce qui use, tout ce qui mord, tout ce qui tue,
Mais ce qui brille tous les jours
C'est l'accord de l'homme et de l'or,
C'est un regard lié à la terre.

Au hasard une délivrance,
Au hasard l'étoile filante
Et l'éternel ciel de ma tête
S'ouvre plus large à son soleil,
A l'éternité du hasard.

By chance

An epic by chance, but now it's finished.
Every act is a prisoner
Of slaves with ancestral beards
And the ordinary words
Are valid only in their memory.

By chance all that burns, all that gnaws,
All that wears down, all that bites, all that kills,
But radiant always
Is the pact of man and gold,
A gaze tied to the earth.

By chance a deliverance, .
By chance a shooting star
And my head's eternal sky
Opens wider to its sun,
To the eternity of chance.

(PT/MAC)

[L'absolute nécessité]

L'absolue nécessité, l'absolu désir, découdre tous ces habits, le plomb de la verdure qui dort sous la feuiliée avec un tapis rouge dans les cheveux d'ordre et de brûlures semant la pâleur, l'azurine de teinte de la poudre d'or du chercheur de noir au fond du rideau dur et renâclant l'humide désertion, poussant le verre ardent, hachure dépendant de l'éternité délirante du pauvre, la machine se disperse et retrouve la ronde armature des rousses au désir de sucre rouge.

Le fleuve se détend, passe avec adresse dans le soleil, regarde la nuit, la trouve belle et à son goût, passe son bras sous le sien et redouble de brutalité, la douceur étant la conjonction d'un œil fermé avec un œil ouvert ou du dédain avec l'enthousiasme, du refus avec la confiance et de la haine avec l'amour, voyez quand même la barrière de cristal que l'homme a fermée devant l'homme, il restera pris par les rubans de sa crinière de troupeaux, de foules, de processions, d'incendies, de semailles, de voyages, de réflexions, d'épopées, de chaînes, de vêtements jetés, de virginités arrachées, de batailles, de triomphes passés ou futurs, de liquides, de satisfactions, de rancunes, d'enfants abandonnés, de souvenirs, d'espoirs, de familles, de races, d'armées, de miroirs, d'enfants de chœur, de chemins de croix, de chemins de fer, de traces, d'appels, de cadavres, de larcins, de pétrifications, de parfums, de promesses, de pitié, de vengeances, de délivrances—dis-je—de délivrances comme au son des clairons ordonnant au cerveau de ne plus se laisser distraire par les masques successifs et féminins d'un hasard d'occasion, aux prunelles des haies, la cavalcade sanglante et plus douce au cœur de l'homme averti de la paix que la couronne des rêves insouciante des ruines du sommeil.

204

[Absolute necessity]

Absolute necessity, absolute desire, to take apart all these clothes, the lead of greenery sleeping under the foliage with a red rug in the hair of order and of burning, sowing the paleness, the blueness of the gold powder of the seeker of darkness in the depths of the hard curtain and scorning the damp desertion, pushing against the burning glass, crosshatching depending on the delirious eternity of the poor, the machine, dispersed, finds once more the round armor of the redheads with their desire of brown sugar.

The stream is at ease, passes skillfully in the sun, gazes at the night, finds it beautiful and to its taste, passes its arm under his and doubles its brutality, gentleness being the meeting of a closed and an open eye, scorn with enthusiasm, refusal with confidence and hatred with love, see how the barrier of crystal that man has closed in front of man, he will remain caught in by the ribbons of his mane of flocks, of crowds, of processions, of fires, of sowings, of voyages, of reflections, of epics, of chains, of castoff clothes, of virginities snatched away, of battles, of triumphs past or to come, of liquids, of satisfactions, of bitterness, of abandoned children, of memories, of hopes, of families, of races, of armies, of mirrors, of choirboys, roads of the cross, of railroads of iron, of traces, of appeals, of corpses, of thefts, of petrifications, of perfumes, of promises, of pity, of vengeance, of deliverance—I say—of deliverance as at the sound of clarions commandanding the brain to no longer let itself be distracted by the successive feminine masks of a chance occasion, commanding the eyes of hedges, the bloody cavalcade sweeter to the heart of the man who knows about peace than the crown of dreams careless of the ruins of sleep.

(MAC)

Entre peu d'autres

A Philippe Soupault.

Ses yeux ont tout un ciel de larmes.
Ni ses paupières, ni ses mains
Ne sont une nuit suffisante
Pour que sa douleur s'y cache.

Il ira demander
Au Conseil des Visages
S'il est encore capable
De chasser sa jeunesse

Et d'être dans la plaine
Le pilote du vent.
C'est une affaire d'expérience:
Il prend sa vie par le milieu.

Seuls, les plateaux de la balance...

Among the happy few

To Philippe Soupault

A sky of tears in his eyes.
Neither his eyelids nor his hands
Make it dark enough
For his pain to hide there.

He will go to ask
The Council of Visages
If he's still capable
Of running after his youth

And of being the pilot of the wind
In the plains
It's a matter of experience:
He takes hold of his life by its middle.

Only the two sides of the scales...

(PT/MAC)

[Revenir dans une ville]

Revenir dans une ville de velours et de porcelaine, les fenêtres seront des vases où les fleurs, qui auront quitté la terre, montreront la lumière telle qu'elle est.

Voir le silence, lui donner un baiser sur les lèvres et les toits de la ville seront de beaux oiseaux mélancoliques, aux ailes décharnées.

Ne plus aimer que la douceur et l'immobilité à l'œil de plâtre, au front de nacre, à l'œil absent, au front vivant, aux mains qui, sans se fermer, gardent tout sur leurs balances, les plus justes du monde, invariables, toujours exactes.

Le cœur de l'homme ne rougira plus, il ne se perdra plus, je reviens de moi-même, de toute éternité.

[To come back to a town]

To come back to a town of velvet and porcelain, the windows will form vases where flowers having left the earth will reveal light as it is.

To see silence, to give it a kiss on the lips and the roofs of the town will be lovely melancholy birds, with bare wings.

To love nothing but sweetness and immobility with an eye of plaster, a forehead of mother-of-pearl, an absent eye, a living forehead, hands which—without closing—hold everything on their scales, the most precise in the world, innvariable, always exact.

The heart of man will no longer blush, will no longer be lost, I return from myself, from all eternity.

(MAC)

Georges Braque

Un oiseau s'envole,
Il rejette les nues comme un voile inutile,
Il n'a jamais craint la lumière,
Enfermé dans son vol,
Il n'a jamais eu d'ombre.

Coquilles des moissons brisées par le soleil.
Toutes les feuilles dans les bois disent oui,
Elles ne savent dire que oui,
Toute question, toute réponse
Et la rosée coule au fond de ce oui.

Un homme aux yeux légers décrit le ciel d'amour.
Il en rassemble les merveilles
Comme des feuilles dans un bois,
Comme des oiseaux dans leurs ailes
Et des hommes dans le sommeil.

Georges Braque

A bird flies away
Throwing off the clouds like a useless veil,
He was never afraid of the light,
Enclosed in his flight,
He's never had a shadow.

Shells of the harvests broken by the sun.
Every leaf in the woods says yes,
All they know how to say is yes,
All questions, all answers
Deep in the yes runs the dew.

A man with weightless eyes describes the sky of love.
He gathers up the wonders of it
Like leaves in a wood,
Like birds in their wings
And people in their sleep.

(MAC/PT)

[Dans la brume]

Dans la brume où des verres d'eau s'entrechoquent, où les serpents cherchent du lait, un monument de laine et de soie disparaît. C'est là que, la nuit dernière, apportant leur faiblesse, toutes les femmes entrèrent. Le monde n'était pas fait pour leurs promenades incessantes, pour leur démarche languissante, pour leur recherche de l'amour. Grand pays de bronze de la belle époque, par tes chemins en pente douce, l'inquiétude a déserté.

Il faudra se passer des gestes plus doux que l'odeur, des yeux plus clairs que la puissance, il y aura des cris, des pleurs, des jurons et des grincements de dents.

Les hommes qui se coucheront ne seront plus désormais que les pères de l'oubli. A leurs pieds le désespoir aura la belle allure des victoires sans lendemain, des auréoles sous le beau ciel bleu dont nous étions parés.

Un jour, ils en seront las, un jour ils seront en colère, aiguilles de feu, masques de poix et de moutarde, et la femme se lèvera, avec des mains dangereuses, avec des yeux de perdition, avec un corps dévasté, rayonnant à toute heure.

Et le soleil refleurira, comme le mimosa.

[In the mist]

In the mist where glasses of water clatter against each other, where snakes come looking for milk, a monument of wool and silk disappears. It is there that, on the last night, bringing their weakness, all the women came in. The world wasn't made for their ceaseless walking around, their langorous gait, their search for love. Great country of bronze of the Belle Epoque, along your paths in their gentle slope, disquiet has deserted.

We'll have to do without gestures sweeter than smell, eyes brighter than power, there will be cries, tears, swearing, and the gnashing of teeth.

The men who lie down will no longer be any more than the fathers of forgetting. At their feet despair will have the lovely aspect of victories with no tomorrow, haloes we put on under the beautiful blue sky.

One day, they will be tired of it, one day they will be angry, needles of fire, masks of pitch and of mustard, and woman will rise, with dangerous hands, with eyes of perdition, with a devastated body, radiant in every moment.

And, the sun will flower once more, like the mimosa.

(MAC)

Les noms: Chéri-Bibi,
Gaston Leroux

Il a dû bien souffrir avec ces oiseaux! Il a pris le goût des animaux, faudra-t-il le manger? Mais il gagne son temps et roule vers le paradis. C'est BOUCHE-DE-CŒUR qui tient la roue et non CHÉRI-BIBI. On le nomme aussi MAMAN, par erreur.

Names: Bibi-Darling,
Gaston Leroux

How he must have suffered from the birds! He developed a taste for animals, must we eat him? But he's gaining time and rolling on toward paradise. It's SWEETHEART-MOUTH at the wheel, and not BIBI-DARLING.

Also called MOM, by mistake.

(NK)

La nuit

Caresse l'horizon de la nuit, cherche le cœur de jais que l'aube recouvre de chair. Il mettrait dans tes yeux des pensées innocentes, des flammes, des ailes et des verdures que le soleil n'inventa pas.

Ce n'est pas la nuit qui te manque, mais sa puissance.

Night

Caress the night's horizon, look for the heart of jet that the dawn covers over with flesh. It would put into your eyes innocent thoughts, flames, wings, and greenery that the sun did not invent.

It isn't the night you are missing, but its power.

(MAC)

Arp

Tourne sans reflets aux courbes sans sourires des ombres à moustaches, enregistre les murmures de la vitesse, la terreur minuscule, cherche sous des cendres froides les plus petits oiseaux, ceux qui ne ferment jamais leurs ailes, résiste au vent.

Arp

Turn without reflecting the unsmiling curves of mustachioed shadows, register murmurs of speed and minuscule terror, seek beneath cold ashes the smallest of birds, those which never fold their wings, resist the wind.

(NK)

Joan Miro

Soleil de proie prisonnier de ma tête,
Enlève la colline, enlève la forêt.
Le ciel est plus beau que jamais.
Les libellules des raisins
Lui donnent des formes précises
Que je dissipe d'un geste.

Nuages du premier jour,
Nuages insensibles et que rien n'autorise,
Leurs graines brûlent
Dans les feux de paille de mes regards.

A la fin, pour se couvrir d'une aube
Il faudra que le ciel soit aussi pur que la nuit.

Joan Miro

Sun prey imprisoned in my head,
Take away the hill, take away the forest.
The sky is more beautiful than ever.
Among the grapes, dragonflies
Bestow on it definite forms
I dispel with a gesture.

Clouds of the first day,
Unfeeling and unauthorised,
Their seeds burn
In the straw fires of my gaze.

In the end, to shelter under a dawn
The sky would have to be as pure as the night.

(PT/MAC)

Jour de tout

Empanaché plat, compagnie et compagnie a la parole facile, tout à dire. Peur plus tiède que le soleil. Il est pâle et sans défauts. Compagnie et compagnie s'est habitué à la lumière.

Est-ce avoir l'air musicien que d'avoir l'air des villes? Il parle, rosés des mots ignorés de la plume.

Et je me dresse devant lui comme le mât d'une tente, et je suis au sommet du mât, colombe.

Everything day

Befeathered and flat, company and easy-talking company, that's saying everything. A fear more tepid than the sun. It is pale and faultless. Company and company have gotten used to the light.

Is looking like a musician the same as looking at ease in cities? He is speaking, in roses of those words unknown to the pen.

And I stand before him like the mast of a tent, and I am at the top of the mast, a dove.

(MAC)

[L'image d'homme]

L'image d'homme, au-dehors du souterrain, resplendit. Des plaines de plomb semblent lui offrir l'assurance qu'elle ne sera plus renversée, mais ce n'est que pour la replonger dans cette grande tristesse qui la dessine. La force d'autrefois, oui la force d'autrefois se suffisait à elle-même. Tout secours est inutile, elle périra par extinction, mort douce et calme.

Elle entre dans les bois épais, dont la silencieuse solitude jette l'âme dans une mer où les vagues sont des lustres et des miroirs. La belle étoile de feuilles blanches qui, sur un plan plus éloigné, semble la reine des couleurs, contraste avec la substance des regards, appuyés sur les troncs de l'incalculable impéritie des végétaux bien accordés.

Au-dehors du souterrain, l'image d'homme manie cinq sabres ravageurs. Elle a déjà creusé la masure où s'abrite le règne noir des amateurs de mendicité, de bassesse et de prostitution. Sur le plus grand vaisseau qui déplace la mer, l'image d'homme s'embarque et conte aux matelots revenant des naufrages une histoire de brigands: « A cinq ans, sa mère lui confia un trésor. Qu'en faire? Sinon de l'amadouer. Elle rompit de ses bras d'enfer la caisse de verre où dorment les pauvres merveilles des hommes. Les merveilles la suivirent. L'œillet de poète sacrifia les cieux pour une chevelure blonde. Le caméléon s'attarda dans une clairière pour y construire un minuscule palais de fraises et d'araignées, les pyramides d'Egypte faisaient rire les passants, car elles ne savaient pas que la pluie désaltère la terre. Enfin, le papillon d'orange secoua ses pépins sur les paupières des enfants qui crurent sentir passer le marchand de sable. »

[The image of man]

The image of man, not now underground, is resplendent. Plains of lead seem to assure him that it will no longer be reversed, but this is only to plunge it again into this great sadness which gives it an outline. The former strength, yes, the former strength used to suffice unto itself. Any succor is useless, it will perish by extinction, a death gentle and calm.

She enters the dense forest, whose silent solitude hurls the soul into a sea whose waves are lamps and mirrors. The lovely star of white leaves that, on a more distant level, seems the queen of the colors, contrasts with the stuff of gazes, leaning on the trunks of the incalculable incompetence, of harmonious plants.

Not now underground, the image of man wields five raging sabers. It has already unearthed the hovel housing the black reign of the enthusiasts of begging, lowliness, and prostitution. On the largest ship displacing the sea, the image of man sets out and recounts to the sailors returning from shipwrecks a story about brigands.: "When he was five, his mother gave him a treasure. What to do with it? Except calm her down. She crushed with her hellish arms the glass container where the poor marvels of man are sleeping. The marvels followed her. The poet's carnation sacrificed the skies for a blonde mane of hair, the chameleon lingered in a clearing to construct there a tiny palace of strawberries and spiders, the Egyptian pyramids made the passersby laugh, because they didn't know that the rains slake the earth's thirst. Finally, the orange butterfly shook its seeds over the eyelids of the children who thought they felt the sandman going by."

L'image d'homme rêve, mais plus rien n'est accroché à ses rêves que la nuit sans rivale. Alors, pour rappeler les matelots à l'apparence de quelque raison, quelqu'un qu'on avait cru ivre prononce lentement cette phrase:

« Le bien et le mal doivent leur origine à l'abus de quelques erreurs. »

The image of man dreams, but nothing more is hanging on his dreams than the unparalleled night. Then, to recall the sailors to some semblance of reason, someone who had seemed drunk slowly uttered this sentence:

"Good and evil have their origin in a few errors carried out to excess."

(MAC)

Le miroir d'un moment

Il dissipe le jour,
Il montre aux hommes les images déliées de l'apparence,
Il enlève aux hommes la possibilité de se distraire.
Il est dur comme la pierre,
La pierre informe,
La pierre du mouvement et de la vue,
Et son éclat est tel que toutes les armures, tous les masques en
    sont faussés.
Ce que la main a pris dédaigne même de prendre la forme de
    la main,
Ce qui a été compris n'existe plus,
L'oiseau s'est confondu avec le vent,
Le ciel avec sa vérité,
L'homme avec sa réalité.

The mirror of a moment

It dispels the day.
It shows us images released from their appearance,
It makes distraction impossible.
It is as hard as stone,
Shapeless stone,
The stone of motion and of sight,
And its brilliance shows all armor, all masks to be false.
What's in the hand disdains to take the shape of the hand,
What's been understood is no more,
The bird and the wind are one,
The sky and its truth,
Ourselves and what is real.

(MAC/PT)

[Ta chevelure d'oranges]

Ta chevelure d'oranges dans le vide du monde
Dans le vide des vitres lourdes de silence
Et d'ombre où mes mains nues cherchent tous tes reflets.

La forme de ton cœur est chimérique
Et ton amour ressemble à mon désir perdu.
O soupirs d'ambre, rêves, regards.

Mais tu n'as pas toujours été avec moi. Ma mémoire
Est encore obscurcie de t'avoir vu venir
Et partir. Le temps se sert de mots comme l'amour.

[Your hair of oranges]

Your hair of oranges in the emptiness of the world
In the emptiness of windowpanes heavy with silence
And shadow where my bare hands seek all your reflections.

Illusory is the shape of your heart
And your love is like my lost desire.
O amber sighs, dreams, gazes.

But you've not always been with me. My memory
Is still darkened from having seen you come
And go. Time uses words like love.

(PT/MAC)

[Les lumières dictées]

Les lumières dictées à la lumière constante et pauvre passent avec moi toutes les écluses de la vie. Je reconnais les femmes à fleur de leurs cheveux, de leur poitrine et de leurs mains. Elles ont oublié le printemps, elles pâlissent à perte d'haleine.

Et toi, tu te dissimulais comme une épée dans la déroute, tu t'immobilisais, orgueil, sur le large visage de quelque déesse méprisante et masquée. Toute brillante d'amour, tu fascinais l'univers ignorant.

Je t'ai saisie et depuis, ivre de larmes, je baise partout pour toi l'espace abandonné.

[The lights dictated]

Comprehensions dictated to the constant poor light pass with me through all the locks of life. I recognize the women by the very surface of their hair, their chest, and their hands. They have forgotten the spring, they are growing pale breathlessly.

And you yourself were hiding like a sword in the retreat, you were motionless, pride, on the broad face of some goddess both scornful and masked. All shining with love, you fascinated the ignorant universe.

I seized you and since then, intoxicated with tears, I embrace everywhere, for you, abandoned space.

(MAC)

[Ta bouche aux lèvres d'or]

Ta bouche aux lèvres d'or n'est pas en moi pour rire
Et tes mots d'auréole ont un sens si parfait
Que dans mes nuits d'années, de jeunesse et de mort
J'entends vibrer ta voix dans tous les bruits du monde.

Dans cette aube de soie où végète le froid
La luxure en péril regrette le sommeil,
Dans les mains du soleil tous les corps qui s'éveillent
Grelottent à l'idée de retrouver leur cœur.

Souvenirs de bois vert, brouillard où je m'enfonce
J'ai refermé les yeux sur moi, je suis à toi,
Toute ma vie t'écoute et je ne peux détruire
Les terribles loisirs que ton amour me crée.

[Your mouth with lips of gold]

Your mouth with lips of gold is not for laughs
And the meaning of your haloed words is so perfect
That in my nights of years, and youth and death
In all the sounds of the world I hear your voice.

In this silken dawn where the cold lingers
Imperiled lust wants to go back to sleep,
In the hands of the sun all the bodies waking
Shiver at the idea of finding their hearts again.

Memories of green wood, fog into which I plunge
I've closed my eyes on myself, I am yours.
My whole life listens to you and I cannot refuse
The terrible leisure your love creates for me.

[Elle est]

Elle est—mais elle n'est qu'à minuit quand tous les oiseaux blancs ont refermé leurs ailes sur l'ignorance des ténèbres, quand la sœur des myriades de perles a caché ses deux mains dans sa chevelure morte, quand le triomphateur se plaît à sangloter, las de ses dévotions à la curiosité, mâle et brillante armure de luxure. Elle est si douce qu'elle a transformé mon cœur. J'avais peur des grandes ombres qui tissent les tapis du jeu et les toilettes, j'avais peur des contorsions du soleil le soir, des incassables branches qui purifient les fenêtres de tous les confessionnaux où des femmes endormies nous attendent.

O buste de mémoire, erreur de forme, lignes absentes, flamme éteinte dans mes yeux clos, je suis devant ta grâce comme un enfant dans l'eau, comme un bouquet dans un grand bois. Nocturne, l'univers se meut dans ta chaleur et les villes d'hier ont des gestes de rue plus délicats que l'aubépine, plus saisissants que l'heure. La terre au loin se brise en sourires immobiles, le ciel enveloppe la vie: un nouvel astre de l'amour se lève de partout—fini, il n'y a plus de preuves de la nuit.

[She is]

She is—she is but only at midnight when all the white birds have closed their wings upon the ignorance of shadows, when the sister of myriad pearls has hidden her hands in her dead hair, when the one who has triumphed delights in sobbing, tired of his devotions to curiosity, the male and brilliant armor of lust. She is so sweet that she has transformed my heart. I was afraid of the great shadows that weave the rugs for the game and the festive costumes, I was afraid of the contortions of the sun in the evening, of the unbreakable branches that purify the windows of all the confessionals where sleeping women await us.

Oh bust of memory, error of form, absent lines, flame extinguished in my closed eyes, I am before your grace like a child in the water, like a bouquet in a great woods. Nocturnal, the universe moves in your warmth and the towns of winter have street gestures more delicate than the hawthorn, more gripping than the moment. The earth in the distance breaks into motionless smiles, the heavens envelop life: a new constellation of love rises from everywhere—finished, there are no more proofs of night.

(NK)

Le grand jour

Viens, monte. Bientôt les plumes les plus légères, scaphandrier de l'air, te tiendront par le cou.

La terre ne porte que le nécessaire et tes oiseaux de belle espèce, sourire. Aux lieux de ta tristesse, comme une ombre derrière l'amour, le paysage couvre tout.

Viens vite, cours. Et ton corps va plus vite que tes pensées, mais rien, entends-tu? rien, ne peut te dépasser.

Broad daylight

Come, climb up. Soon the lightest feathers, diver of air, will hold you by the neck.

The earth only bears what is essential and your birds of fine sort, a smile. In the places of your sadness, like a shadow behind love, the landscape covers everything.

Come quickly, run. And your body moves more quickly than your thoughts, but nothing, do you hear? nothing can surpass you.

(MAC)

[La courbe de tes yeux]

La courbe de tes yeux fait le tour de mon cœur,
Un rond de danse et de douceur,
Auréole du temps, berceau nocturne et sûr,
Et si je ne sais plus tout ce que j'ai vécu
C'est que tes yeux ne m'ont pas toujours vu.

Feuilles de jour et mousse de rosée,
Roseaux du vent, sourires parfumés,
Ailes couvrant le monde de lumière,
Bateaux chargés du ciel et de la mer,
Chasseurs des bruits et sources des couleurs

Parfums éclos d'une couvée d'aurores
Qui gît toujours sur la paille des astres,
Comme le jour dépend de l'innocence
Le monde entier dépend de tes yeux purs
Et tout mon sang coule dans leurs regards.

[The shape of your eyes]

The shape of your eyes goes around my heart,
A round of dance and sweetness.
Halo of time, cradle nocturnal and sure
No longer do I know what I've lived,
Your eyes have not always seen me.

Leaves of day and moss of dew,
Reeds of wind and scented smiles,
Wings lighting up the world,
Boats laden with sky and sea,
Hunters of sound and sources of color,

Scents the echoes of a covey of dawns
Recumbent on the straw of stars,
As the day relies on innocence
The world depends on your pure sight
All my blood courses in its glance.

Celle de toujours, toute

Si je vous dis: « j'ai tout abandonné »
C'est qu'elle n'est pas celle de mon corps,
Je ne m'en suis jamais vanté,
Ce n'est pas vrai
Et la brume de fond où je me meus
Ne sait jamais si j'ai passé.

L'éventail de sa bouche, le reflet de ses yeux,
Je suis le seul à en parler,
Je suis le seul qui soit cerné
Par ce miroir si nul où l'air circule à travers moi
Et l'air a un visage, un visage aimé,
Un visage aimant, ton visage,
A toi qui n'as pas de nom et que les autres ignorent,
La mer te dit: sur moi, le ciel te dit: sur moi,
Les astres te devinent, les nuages t'imaginent
Et le sang répandu aux meilleurs moments,
Le sang de la générosité
Te porte avec délices.
Je chante la grande joie de te chanter,
La grande joie de t'avoir ou de ne pas t'avoir,
La candeur de t'attendre, l'innocence de te connaître,

O toi qui supprimes l'oubli, l'espoir et l'ignorance,
Qui supprimes l'absence et qui me mets au monde,
Je chante pour chanter, je t'aime pour chanter
Le mystère où l'amour me crée et se délivre.

Tu es pure, tu es encore plus pure que moi-même.

242

Forever, entirely

If I tell you: "I've given up everything"
It's that she's not part of my body,
I've never boasted of it,
It isn't true
And the fog in the depths where I travel
Never knows if I've gone by.

The fan of her mouth, the brilliance of her eyes,
I'm the only one to speak of it,
I'm the only one framed
By this mirror so empty the air flows through me
And the air has a face, a beloved face,
A loving face, your face,
To you nameless and to the others, unknown,
The sea tells you: on me, the sky tells you: on me,
The stars find you out, the clouds imagine you
And blood spilled in the best moments,
The blood of generosity
Bears you with delight.
I sing the great joy of singing you,
The great joy of having you or not having you,
The candor of awaiting you, the innocence of knowing you,

Oh! You put an end to forgetfulness, ignorance, hope,
You put an end to absence, give birth to me,
I sing in order to sing, I love you in order to sing
The mystery by which love creates me and is set free.

You are pure, you are even purer than I.

(PT/MAC)

ESSAY ON ELUARD'S POETRY

Mary Ann Caws

Capital of Pain illustrates some of the same elements which will remain true of Eluard's poetry in all of its phases. The same themes of purity, spontaneity, and intensity which are of major importance in Tristan Tzara's Dada manifestos and Andre Breton's surrealist declarations pervade all the writings of Eluard—poetry and prose, early and late. It is true that the "absolute liberty" he continues to champion after his break with surrealism does not, as it did at first, insist on the idealistic requirement stated in *La Révolution surréaliste* (No.3): "no word will ever again be subordinated to matter." But the new framework of political interpretation does not alter in any way Eluard's tone or his imagery. This continuity is perfectly understandable when one reads in his *Anthologie des écrits sur l'art* such quotations from the young Marx as: "The essential form of wit is gaiety, light,"[1] "Art is the highest joy man can offer himself."[2]

Eluard's own poetry does not change, nor does his definition of poetry. Poetic fidelity, he says in his preface to *La Poésie du passé* (1951), requires clarity of vision, reflection of that vision, and action: it requires "keeping your eyes open on yourself and on the world, on the front of the mirror and on the back of the mirror in order to hold off the night." The vocabulary and the concepts are much the same as they were twenty years earlier, with an emphasis on light, on the image with its metamorphosing power, and on the future community of all people, united in a common vision: "Weak man transforms himself into radiant man .... The image is his

244

virtue. He dissolves himself and gives himself a new form, he knows how to live and to bestow life, he is common."[3] Now, of course, we recognize how appropriate is this vision to that of his political commitment. in any case, each of the main elements salient in this passage is essential to the whole of Eluard's system of values: the luminosity of the new (surrealist) vision, the potential self-transformation of poets by their vision and the necessity of sharing it.

"Radiant man" applies to all beings who refuse to limit themselves to the old world of reason, which Eluard considers a dull and disordered world. Poets and painters, the "ordonnateurs," see a new bright and irrational order in things, an order which their vision reinforces. The natural and luminous arrangement Eluard values clearly contrasts with the tempestuous *ordre* of Dada: "We admire the order of things, the order of rocks, the order of hours. But this shadow which disappears and this sorrowful element which disappears."[4] Here in Eluard's new view, the observer does not impose the narrowing grid of a rational interpretation on the simplicity of nature. The lost contact between the object perceived and the mind perceiving is reestablished as artists see everything afresh and, offering the vision to others, double the clarity for themselves: "Que fleurisse ton oeil / Lumière" (I, 579) / (Let your eye flower / Light). The motto *donner à voir* is not an empty oral pun; it is equally valid in its two meanings ("to give to have" and "to offer vision"). To see and comprehend clearly and to help others see and comprehend is the highest possible achievement. Furthermore, seeing and understanding are equivalent for Eluard: *"voir, c'est comprendre"* (I, 526).[5] So, for him, there is no gap between the visual and the mental. His poetic theories are all based on this simplicity of sight and thought and on this union or reunion of disparate or disordered elements: "J'établis des rapports . . . ."[6] Such relationships (*rapports*) as he establishes apply to the human as well as to the object world: linking the elements of one, he links those of the other. The search for a "fil conducteur" or a conducting wire, a bridge over the gap, is a common aspiration for all the surrealists.

In "Le Miroir de Baudelaire" (*Minotaure*, 1, 1933), Eluard discusses the poetic technique of comparison, the surrealist technique *par excellence,* and warns that the power to compare is not to be taken for granted by all poets since the resemblance between two things is determined more by the character of the mind that perceives it than by the objective relationship that may exist or be *created.* (If he had used the verb "identify" instead of the verb "establish" in describing the role played by the poet in making the comparison, he would have implied that the resemblance was certain, in which case the image would not demand the effort essential to surrealism. For the surrealist image cannot be simply stated by the poet or passively observed by the reader; they must both actively participate in it, even if the action is spontaneous and subconscious.)

Like Tristan Tzara, Eluard considers poetry a form of constant motion. Participation precedes comprehension: "All that really matters is to participate, to move, to understand."[7] Only someone actively engaged in the surrounding world with the whole force of an imaginative vision is able to escape a paralyzing solitude, accepting an active responsibility for others. The poet who is "on earth" cannot take a safe distance from the suffering of others but must participate in it:

> Où donc est la muraille poétique du bien-être
> Que nous la renversions
> Et que nous prenions pied dans ce monde impossible[8]

> (where then is the poetic wall of well-being
> So we can knock it down
> And take a stand in this impossible world).

In his *L'Avenir de la poésie* (1937) Eluard points out as Baudelaire's most significant contribution his realization that the "I" always points to an "us," that ultimately poetry should depend on a universal equality of happiness. Here the last two points of Eluard's poetic program are clarified and united. As the poet *realizes* or *creates* the unlikely resemblance which is the image he recreates himself, the observer, and the whole community of men—that is, he makes himself "common." In this sense poetry is not, as Eluard says once more in *Les Sentiers et routes de la poesie,* an object of art, limited to personal aesthetic enjoyment, but an *object to be used,* a conception based on Lautreamont's dictum so often quoted by the surrealists: "Personal poetry has had its age . . . " The dark images of individual uselessness should yield to the bright ones of a common universe: "And the good of all men has no shadow."[9]

In his *Anthologie des écrits sur l'art* (1952), Eluard expresses the hope that drawing will some day become a social fact like language and writing, and that eventually all the forms of communication will pass from the trivial social plane to the universal plane on which "all men will communicate by the vision of things and they will use this vision to express the point that is common to them, to them and to things, to them as it is to things, to things as it is to them."[10] His old formula: "voir, c'est comprendre" is now expanded: "To see is to understand and to act; to see is to unite the world with man and man with man."[11] Those separated in an epoch of moral misery, and artists like Picasso understand that the most essential task is to encourage the enthusiasm that can unite them in a new and optimistic perception. Picasso, better than anyone else, is able to demonstrate a "poetic reason" for the infinite series of relationships he sees between things which is the artistic equivalent of the childlike vision. Adult or logical thought makes a sharp distinction between concrete things and their abstract relations, whereas animals and primitive man, insane persons and children, immediately establish simple emotional relationships based on sympathy and antipathy. But their instinctive power of comparison is the only alternative to the alienating or civilized rational age. The ideal vision presented by the poet approximates the prerational instinct of a child who sees and understands simultaneously, in an immediacy strange to the "normal" sensibility of the adult mind. This natural poetic closeness to creation is the answer to the physical and mental human isolation. It is no more difficult for the poet of the marvelous to make a fire in the snow than to "blend the swimmer with the river" as Picasso does. In an essay on Max Ernst, Eluard speaks of the artist's power to transmute everything into everything else, and the strength of his own poetry is based on exactly that power. Following the principle enunciated by Breton[12] that in our world the aspects of all things are open and therefore interchangeable, Eluard sees one woman as a hundred and any object as any other: on this openness of vision depends the sense of multiplicity essential to his poetic universe, his consciousness of the "multiplied dimensions of future strength" (I, 1101). Each separate object, valuable in itself ("L'unique soleil") contains an unlimited potentiality of expansion: "Une seule goutte d'eau / Multipliait ses haloes" (II, 431) / (A single drop of water / Multiplied its haloes). From "une aurore unique" comes a succession of days. All things are *ressemblantes* in the poetic perspective, and so they repeat each other in an endless series of reflections: a town can be "repeated" like a poem, because it resembles." Eluard does not specify what it resembles, since to specify would be to limit, while the goal of his poetry and of surrealist poetry in general is to go beyond the limits.

All relationships between things, no matter how modest, are flexible and infinite, infinitely generative of new forms of vision. If a tiny bird walks "dans d'immenses régions", the sun is likely to sprout wings. In Eluard's poetry, water forms hills and men inebriate the wine; there are no fixed frameworks. Through the principles of constant transference and uninterrupted communication, the world of nature expands the human world:

Les arbres nous grandissaient (I, 47)

(The trees enlarged us).

To an even greater extent than Breton, Eluard occupies himself with a poetic investigation of the paradox "one within the other." Breton wants his life and works to have the spontaneous brilliance of the crystal, but Eluard values above all else *La Vie immédiate*, that is, "to participate, to move, to understand," being not separate but rather *ressemblant*, to perceive things not as discontinuous, but as joined. In an early essay on Ernst, Eluard describes the insepa- rable nature of the exterior and the interior, of "matter, movement, need, desire."[13] There is no distance between man and the objects of his vision, and ideally none between things actual and imagined, the concrete and the abstract: they are in fact identified with each other. This belief is sometimes reflected in a continual telescoping of images, as in the poem "Cœur à pic" (from *Cours naturel*), where human images are mixed with natural ones:

> Villages peuples eau pleine
> . . .
> Lampes de pain enfants de feuilles

> (Towns of people water full
> . . .
> Lamps of bread children of leaves),

where the abstract powers of language and vision, as well as intan- gible feelings, are identified with the physical landscape:

> Moulins des miroirs et des yeux
> Iles des seins sillons des mots
> Neige câline de la force
> Mares fanées de la fatigue

> (Windmills of mirrors and eyes
> Islands of breasts furrows of words
> Caressing snow of strength
> Faded ponds of fatigue).

This poem is genuinely a meeting-place of the dissimilar and the contrary, since phrases of fullness, abundance, light, and strength join those of secrecy, darkness, and disaster in a permanent poetic union, effectively illustrating Eluard's desire that the "transparent image" should reflect and be a reflection of the *point confluent* at the heart of the real.

Art is the principle of exaltation, but also of participation and transformation: one of the highest compliments Eluard pays to an artist is his description of Dominguez's work as "lofty paintings hot with metamorphosis." To accept seriously the basic principles of *ressemblance* and interchangeability implies the acceptance of a further, more difficult irrationality—that a man can be at once his own being and another:

> Je fus rocher dans l'homme l'homme dans le rocher
> Je fus oiseau dans l'air espace dans l'oiseau[14]

> (I was a rock in man man within the rock
> I was a bird in air space within the bird).

The imaginative ability bestowed on poets to identify themselves with what they see is no more important than the psychological capability of transforming oneself into a different personality, of recreating oneself entirely through the "mediation of all beings."

> Je suis le spectateur et l'acteur et l'auteur
> Je suis la femme et son mari et leur enfant
> . . .
> Car où commence un corps je prends forme et conscience
> Et même quand un corps se défait dans la mort
> Je gis en son creuset j'épouse son tourment[15]

> (I am the spectator and the actor and the author
> I am the woman and her husband and their child
> . . .
> For where there is a body I take on form and consciousness
> And even when a body is undone in death
> I lie in its crucible I wed its torment).

A poet's consciousness begins with the consciousness of every other being, a poet's form begins with any other form. What is stylistic condensation or juxtaposition in Tzara's transcription of the natural world becomes, in Eluard's, a deliberate suppression of *personal* distance, which leaves the space of the poem untouched. The unceasing metamorphosis of the individual, and of individuals together, is the primary manifestation of what Eluard calls *La Poésie ininterrompue* of the "undivided world" ("le monde sans rupture").
See also his *Poésie ininterrompue:*

> Je suis ma mère et mon enfant
>
> . . .
>
> Je suis mon rayon de soleil
> Et je suis mon bonheur nocturne. (II, 26)

> (I am my mother and my child
>
> . . .
>
> I am the ray of my own sun
> And I am my nighttime happiness.)

This vision rests on the denial of separation and on the absolute power of poetry. For Eluard, as for all the surrealists, the poet creates his own past and his own space: "j'avais mon paysage et je m'y suis perdue" (I, 1199)[16] / (I had my landscape and lost myself there). He wills a vision of constant motion in the universe equivalent to the human hope "of always being mobile." (II, 898) The most valuable images or objects are those capable of forming a "moving mirror" for a writer or reader, a recollection of motion and an inspiration for a constant becoming. Breton's concise statement: "Always for the first time" has an exact parallel in Eluard's credo" "To be at the beginning," or "The celebration is always new," and the leitmotif running through Eluard's poems—"Grandir est sans limites" (I, 406) / (Growing is limitless)—is the *ideal* of surrealism itself. When space and time are annulled by poetic reality or surreality, there is no limit to the force of surrealist poetry, to the field of surrealist vision, or to the faith of surrealist love. At the height of this faith, every poet can claim that the lover and the beloved are future, that all poets are "en avant," and that in the world surrounding them, "rien n'a des limites" (I, 124) / (nothing has limits).

One might expect at least the concept of nonlimitation to be without shadow. But there is an opposite perception even here, and it arises not in the exterior world, but in the inherent human reluctance to accept unlimited possibility. Eluard's confession is, as always, simply phrased because it is meant for everyone who has or has once had his confidence in the potentiality of poetry:

Je souffre d'être sans limites. (II 681)

(I suffer from being limitless.)

Eluard is so naturally a poet that he states his theories of art more convincingly in his poems themselves than in any of his prose writings. His notion of the image as a "perfect contact" and as a "confluent point," of the poet as the double of the beings he observes and whose truth he guarantees, and as the person uniquely responsible for the spiritual and actual inventory of the real ("Tout dire," "Je rends compte du réel," "Et je veux dire ce qui est")—these form an integral part of his verse. They *are* poetry as much as they are reflections upon it, in the same way as the reflection of love implies a parallel identification. All Eluard's theories are mingled in a relationship which endlessly mirrors the aim of poetry or of art, an aim of multiplicity, expansion, and endless communication.[17] It is hard not to see this refusal to stand outside his own poems, this quiet integration of theory and poetry, as a further example of his basic modesty and understatement, the necessary and oddly touching opposite (or double) of his requirement that poetry have the volume of a shout of joy, and the irreversible force of a wave.

In *Cours naturel* (1938), a title that indicates a certain acceptance of things as they are, Eluard meditates at length on the language which is the point of contact between the order of man and the order of the world, on its value and on the realm of poetic creation which is as unlimited as the realm of vision. All words are marvelous by their nature, all are *equivalent*. For Eluard, the poet's task is also to make equivalents of all possible questions, their answers and their echoes. Poetry is a principle of balance ("ma limite et mon infini") and a realm of potential rearrangement over which it is the poet's privilege to reign:

> O mon empire d'homme
> Mots que j'écris ici
> Contre toute évidence[18]

> (O my empire of man
> Words that I write here
> In the face of all the facts).

The structures a poet controls in his language exert a powerful influence over the natural elements; at the "first limpid word," material obstacles and awkwardness disappear to make way for the constantly renewed possibility of a fresh and even facile beginning in clarity.

"Image, oh perfect contact . . . "—along with the consciousness of multiplicity runs a parallel consciousness of immediacy; the contact between the object and the person who sees it to be reestablished so that poets are in no way separate from the surrounding world. They have the power to create a special universe outside themselves, and contrary to all usual perception ("Tonight I shall build an exceptional night / Mine"), reflecting their own vision like a perfect mirror, multiplying each personal image and creating a sense of community. The most perfect example of this ideal (and perhaps also real) community and its poetic vision of liberation is expressed in the often-quoted and majestic poem "Sans âge," also from *Cours naturel*. Entirely constructed about the themes of creation, fraternity, childlike innocence and freshness, and around the parallel images of purity and light, joy, warmth, and language, "Sans âge" can be read either as a poem about surrealism or about Communist fraternity, or about the fraternity of poets, or better still as an example of the similarity between all three:

Nous approchons
Dans les forêts

Prenez la rue du matin
Montez marches de la brume

Nous approchons
La terre en a le coeur crispé
Encore un jour à mettre au monde.

———

Le ciel s'élargira
Nous en avions assez
D'habiter dans les ruines du sommeil
Dans l'ombre basse du repos
De la fatigue de l'abandon

La terre reprendra la forme de nos corps vivants
Le vent nous subira
Le soleil et la nuit passeront dans nos yeux
Sans jamais les changer

Notre espace certain notre air pur est de taille
A combler le retard creusé par l'habitude
Nous aborderons tous une mémoire nouvelle
Nous parlerons ensemble un langage sensible.

———

O mes frères contraires gardant dans vos prunelles
La nuit infuse et son horreur

. . .

Moi je vais vers la vie j'ai l'apparence d'homme
Pour prouver que le monde est fait à ma mesure

Et je ne suis pas seul
Mille images de moi multiplient ma lumière
Mille regards pareils égalisent la chair
C'est l'oiseau c'est l'enfant c'est le roc c'est la plaine
Qui se mêlent à nous
L'or éclate de rire de se voir hors du gouffre
L'eau le feu se dénudent pour une seule saison
Il n'y a plus d'éclipse au front de l'univers

———

. . .

Le prisme respire avec nous
Aube abondante

Au sommet de chaque herbe reine
Au sommet des mousses à la pointe des neiges
Des vagues des sables bouleversés
Des enfances persistantes
Hors de toutes les cavernes
Hors de nous-mêmes[19]

———

We draw nearer
In the forests
Take the street of morning
Climb the steps of mist

We draw nearer
The earth is impatient

Once more a day to be born.

———

The sky will open out
We were tired
Of living in the ruins of sleep
In the lowly shadows of rest
Of fatigue of abandon
The earth will assume once more the form of our living bodies
The wind will submit to us
Sun and night will pass into our eyes
Never changing them

Our certain space our pure air is sufficient
To fill the delay dug by habit
We will all begin a new memory
We will speak a sensitive language together.

———

O my contrary brothers holding in your eyes
The night infused with horror

. . .

I move toward life I have the look of man
To prove that the world is made to my measure

Furthermore, each poem has a section (not quoted) in which the village of doubting and impurity is abandoned by the poetic hero: "We have forever / left behind us hope that exhausts itself / In a town fashioned of flesh and of misery"; "Where have I left you / With your hands in the lazy oil / Of your former deeds / With so little hope that death wins out/ Oh my lost brothers."

Jean-Pierre Richard in his brilliant commentary on Eluard (*Onze études sur la poésie moderne* [Seuil, 1964], underlines many other dualities than those mentioned here. He speaks for instance, of the virgin moments which are totally offered, of the light abolished and recreated, of the objects both illuminated and illuminating. And in his interpretation of "Sans âge," he stresses the opposition between the "pointe" and the expression "hors de," an opposition which reveals Eluard's passion at once for the finite and for the open.

> And I am not alone
> A thousand of my images multiply my light
> A thousand similar gazes equalize the flesh
> The bird the child the rock the plain
> Mingle with us
> The gold laughs to find itself outside the chasm
> Water fire bare themselves for a single season
> There is no more eclipse on the forehead of the universe
> ———
>
> . . .
> The prism breathes with us
> Abundant dawn
> Queen at the point of each grass blade
> At the summit of moss at the peak of snow
> Waves sands overturned
> Lasting childhoods
> Outside all caves
> Outside ourselves.)

In this setting of absolute activity, man is stronger even than the nature which surrounds him ("le vent nous subira") and the force of the poem is entirely dependent on the theme of human confidence. The vocabulary is one of *approach* and never of distance, of birth and rebirth, where death enters only in the picture of the "frères contraires," their hands weighed down with the heaviness of an unforgettable past—they are unable to undertake a new beginning. All the elements of this poem are equal to each other, or "ressem-blants," man and bird, rock and plain, sand and snow, prism and cavern, the point of the grass blade and the texture of moss. When the divisiveness of space is overcome, size and categories have no function. The occasional startling image ("A la pointe des neiges") is swallowed up in the simple progression of the whole poem as it moves from consciousness of self to freedom and fraternity. The innocent revolution against habit and outgrown language and toward the positive integration of the natural with the human ("C'est le roc c'est la plaine / Qui se mêlent a nous") are exactly in accordance with Eluard's idea of art, which requires that the elements and man be set a liberty and renewed in clarity. The atmosphere of purity and expansion is so intense that even the basic elements must throw off their outer covering ("l'eau et le feu se dénudent") but the sense of unique revelation is so strong that it cannot occur twice ("pour une seule saison"). Of course these last two qualities are, in another framework, the constituent qualities of the litanic form, which is at once naked (bare repetition) and forever new, each phrase starting from a fresh though single beginning: that is, what is often seen as repetition and elaboration is, if one looks at it from the other side, unique and simple.

This poem should be compared and contrasted with Tzara's *L'Homme Approximatif* (*Approximate Man*). Although both describe pilgrimages, Eluard's poem is directed toward perfect vision and Tzara's, toward perfect language. The final purification of *L'Homme approximatif* takes place in bare and ascetic surroundings (rocks, desert, flame), and the perfection itself is spiritually difficult and physically austere ("up there all is stone"), while the movement in which Eluard participates is an ascent toward a full, harmonious, and yet facile communion of all human and natural elements, closer to Tzara's later poems of "plénitude." Both journeys depend on the human will, but Tzara's is lonelier. His solitary hero of language finally rejects the help of the shepherd who would guide him, and although he is repeatedly likened to all of us and even to those who preferred to reject language ("comme moi comme toi comme les autres silences"), at the end, when the poet has identified himself completely with his hero, he is alone in the desert. Eluard denies any solitude for the poet ("et je ne suis pas seul"), and in the final step of the journey, the poet and his companions transcend all personal limits ("hors de nous-mêmes"). Tzara's epic, through an immense and lengthy effort of language, moves toward a final inwardness, and Eluard's, in a narrower linguistic range, toward a final expansion.

It is clear that poetry "sans age" can, in this context, no longer be the whispered and intimate communication of merely personal sentiment. To reflect these universal similarities and to make moral or active statements, only poetry of deliberate outward expansion is appropriate. Always conscious, like Aragon, of his own poetry and of the tone he wants to give it, Eluard speaks of his poems as *Le Livre ouvert* (1940), and to act of writing he now applies the verb "Crier":

Je me mets à crier
Chacun parlait trop bas parlait et écrivait
Trop bas

(I begin to shout
Everyone was speaking too softly speaking and writing
Too softly).

The poet must create a language larger than himself, that will precede him and extend his horizons; in fact Eluard often identifies language with the path itself.

But even at the height of the optimism in *Cours naturel,* where, by a further extension, he can say of himself and his fellow poets, "Et nous menons partout" (I, 805) / (And we lead everywhere), he suddenly envisions all paths as frozen and silent and an hour stopped in a horrible immobility, denying the natural course of events as well as the power of the poet. Just to perceive the interdependence of dualities ("Et le printemps est dans l'hiver") is far less difficult than the personal experience of them the poet is forced to undergo: "Je brûle et je gêle à jamais" (I, 686) / (I burn and I freeze forever). Yet neither sensitivity nor experience is enough: the poet must also sacrifice all his pleasure in the aesthetic complexities of feeling and expression to the optimistic and sometimes blatant public language of crescendo, so that "les frissons délicats feront place à la houle" (the delicate shivers give way to the great wave). All the stress falls on the necessary simplification of poetry which miraculously (or naturally) conveys the multiplicity of vision and experience: "Ici l'action se simplifie . . . "; "Ecrire simplicité lui-même."

Pouvoir tout dire (1951) contains a summation of Eluard's fully developed poetic theory with its wholehearted faith in reality, community, and regeneration: "Plus rien ne nous fera douter de ce poème / Que j'écris aujourd'hui pour effacer hier." As all the actions of yesterday are wiped out by the presence of poetry, so all the distances of solitude and strangeness are effaced, and no one will ever again have to speak "une langue étrangère." But the faith in poetry is accompanied this time by a genuine modesty. All the limits outside the poet have been erased, and still the poet senses an interior limit he will never overcome: "Le tout est de tout dire et je manque de mots" (II, 363) / (All that matters is to say everything, and I lack words). The realization of the limits of language does not, however, provoke the anguish felt in Tzara's long poem; it would never serve as the emotional basis for an epic.

Profoundly different from the overwhelming, if temporary, self-confidence of 1938 which permitted Eluard to claim that the world was made to his measure, is the quiet and touching "Cinquième poème visible" of 1947, where the poet, ageless as ever, but increasingly haunted by the images of death, is thankful that he can continually give birth to a poetry which will "fit the earth." He creates bright images to balance the inevitable dark ones imposed by human circumstances and acknowledges that the earth is enough for him, even though it is no longer seen as adjusting itself to human desires. In the same way that Tzara builds his late poetry on the concepts of *plénitude* and what is *juste*, Eluard accepts the "real" limits of earth for man's accomplishments and matches his creations to its outlines. (And it is in exactly this context that he and Tzara abandon in their later poetry the surrealistic attitude which is made to no measure.) Eluard does not picture himself now as striding out from a forest, dominating the wind, or leaving his human form behind. The assurance he feels is more natural than it is exalted: "Je suis sur terre et tout est sur terre avec moi" (II, 157) / (I am on earth and everything is on earth with me).

*   *   *

Of all the surrealist and ex-surrealist poets, Eluard is unquestion-ably the clearest in his poetry and in his vision. For that reason he has been able to give, as he says himself, a perfect form to his joy and his poetic understanding. His poems are more elemental than subtle and more lyric than profound, which is as appropriate for a poet of the people as it is for a "frère voyant" in the community of artist and poet visionaries.

Poetry is, for Eluard as for Tristan Tzara, "the art of light." It is at the same time clarity of vision, and an ordering of the real and the imaginary into a fresh consciousness of clarity. In an essay on the art-ist Jacques Villon, Eluard contrasts the "nocturnals" of art like Caravag-gio, Rembrandt, and Goya, whose paintings show "wounded forms in an imperiled world," with the "diurnals" like Piero della Francesca, Poussin, Ingres, Seurat, and Villon, whose paintings imitate the sun, bestowing "heat, order, and clarity" and replacing anguish with lucidity.[20] The moment of ecstasy or total equilibrium reigns forever in the work of Villon, which celebrates the visible world in all its radiant unity. Here light is "the angel of geometry," the principle of rhythmic relationships, a perfect manifestation of eternity. But Villon never turns away from the concrete world toward pure abstraction. Eluard points out that his paint-ings after 1935 are full of harvests, of bread and wine; they represent, in their primary structure, a simple generosity and a genuine, uncompli-cated contact with the earth which is akin to Tzara's plénitude.

"I am the twin of the beings I love," claims Eluard, and in fact his own poetry is famous for the same qualities he distinguishes in Villon's painting. All his optimistic poems, early and late, share this atmosphere of warmth, work, order, and clarity. They are all stamped, as are the brighter poems of Tzara, with the images of fire and sun which are already present in his first poems, where he expresses the desire which remains with him all his life, that of having the sun as a witness to his constant mobility: ("Le soleil me suit/ the sun follows me"),[21] and an inspiration to his own *vertige*, where he declares his faithfulness to the crystalline and luminous world of the poet ("Clarté des moyens employés / Vitre Claire").[22]

One of the short poems of the early *Les Nécessities de la vie* (1921) demonstrates the calm enumeration and awareness of totality familiar in the poetry of Reverdy and in Eluard's own later poems. The possible melancholy of its title, "Enfermé, seul," is contradicted by each of the six lines and by their harmony:

> Chanson complète,
> La table à voir, la chaise pour s'asseoir
> Et l'air à respirer.
> Se reposer,
> Idée inévitable,
> Chanson complète.

> (Complete song,
> The table to see, the chair to sit in
> And the air to breathe.
> To rest,
> Inevitable idea,
> Complete song.)

But in the same collection there is a remarkable prose poem, dedicated to Tzara, which summarizes in its brevity a strange and pathetic movement from the Dada ideals of activity, purity, and dynamic "order" through a sobering contact with reality—the initial optimism of the voyage ("aller et retour") is canceled out by images of a long passageway lined with dirty children and empty bags, and by the reddened eyes of the traveler—toward the final unhealthy images of fatigue and despair:

> L'aube tombée comme une douche. Les coins de la salle sont loin et solides. Plan blanc . . . .Façons-erreurs. Grand agir deviendra nu miel malade, mal jeu déjà sirop, tête noyée, lassitude.

> (Dawn fallen like a shower. The corners of the room are distant and solid. Overall white . . . . Manners-errors. Great

activity will become naked sick honey, wrong game already syrup, drowned head, lassitude.)

Thus the well-planned, necessary, precise beauty of the *gesture* ends in the soft and sticky, even liquid surroundings which threaten any future action or thought. Exhaustion mocks the former hope of accomplishment, as the sickly honey mocks the former solidity and the order of the room "sans mélange." This is a short, and perfect, example of the destruction of a prose poem by itself, a sort of pilgrimage in reverse; and in this self-negation, the poem is Dada.

There could not be two more opposed attitudes than those revealed in these examples; this striking alternation of despair and contentment will always be characteristic of Eluard's vision and of the poetry which it determines: "Je voulus chanter l'ombre" / (I wanted to sing the shadow); "Et pourtant j'ai su chanter le soleil" / (and yet I have been able to sing the sun).

An excerpt from *Défense de savoir* in a 1927 issue of *La Révolution surréaliste* takes the place among Eluard's poems held by the poem of despair and ennui among those of Breton and Tzara. It makes a quiet and moving statement on the poet's feeling of falsity and poetic impotence:

> Ma presence n'est pas ici.
> Je suis habillé de moi-même.
>   . . .
> La clarté existe sans moi.
> Née de ma main sur mes yeux
> Et me détournant de ma voie
> L'ombre m'empêche de marcher
> Sur ma couronne d'univers,
> Dans le grand miroir habitable,
> Miroir brisé, mouvant, inverse
> Où l'habitude et la surprise
> Créent l'ennui à tour de rôle.

(My presence is not here.
I am dressed in myself.

. . .

Brightness exists without me.

Born of my hand over my eyes
And turning me aside from my path
The shadow keeps me from walking
On the crown of the universe.
In the great livable mirror,
Broken mirror, moving, inverted
Where habit and surprise
Alternately create tedium.)

When the poet loses his sense of immediacy and necessity in the world ("La clarté existe sans moi"), the bright surface of the mirror which reflected his genuine images is replaced by the artificial and empty appearance of an image ("habillé de moi-même") and the misleading obscurity for which the poet realizes he is somehow responsible ("née de ma main"). As is the case with most surrealist poetry and theory, the image is contemporary with and absolutely inseparable from the poet's feeling: it is neither a prediction nor a by-product. The image of a broken mirror in Eluard is itself the basis of a whole poem and is never an elaboration of a prior sentiment of confusion.

But in other parts of *Défense de savoir*, the poet has sufficient strength to deny all knowledge ("carcasses of the known"), all "illusions of memory," and all experience in order to assert his own present power over the world:

Et je soumets le monde dans un miroir noir

. . .

Je suis au cœur du temps et je cerne l'espace. (I, 218)
(And I dominate the world in a black mirror

. . .

I am at the center of time and I surround space.)

This last line reflects once more the surrealist aspiration to a *point sublime*, the center and the circumference of the universe, where even contradictions as this are resolved. Compare Breton's image of "The man immobile at the center of the whirlwind," and his lines: "Je suis au centre des choses / Je tiens le fil." The real world is filled up ("comblé") by the shadowy double for the poet, who conquers both the clarity of the mirror and the laws of time and space:

Regarde-moi
La perspective ne joue pas pour moi
Je tiens ma place (I, 297)

(Look at me
Perspective does not work in my case
I remain where I am).

His prideful solitude is based on an absolute self-assurance.

But in *A toute épreuve* (1930) the poet recognizes with sadness rather than pride "everything that separates a man from himself / The loneliness of all beings." In the long poem "Univers-solitude" found in this 1930 collection, the despair is at its extreme point; the accustomed transparency of the poet's connection with the world is interrupted. And all the exterior light which usually accompanies it has been exhausted. There is no vitality, and no communication:

La vie s'est affaissée mes images sont sourdes
. . .
Je suis seul je suis seul tout seul
Je n'ai jamais changé. (I, 297)
. . .

(Life has given way my images are deaf
. . .
I am alone alone completely alone
I have never changed.)

Worse even than the forbidding aspect of the outside world and the personal solitude of the poet is the sudden annihilation of his capacity for art, which could ordinarily save him: the most pathetic confession poets can make does not concern themselves, but rather their creation—"mes images sont sourdes." And again, in the same collection, all the simple confidence in poetic communication returns with an unaffected faith in the present moment:

> La simplicité même écrire
> Pour aujourd'hui la main est là.

> (Simplicity itself to write
> At least today the hand is there.)

Later, in *La Rose publique* of 1934, the poet is once more subject to the same overwhelming despair and emptiness. The calm garden where he used to work alone with the sun burning his hands now becomes "an island without animals," disconnected from reality, inhabited only by an endless consciousness of the unreliability of individual judgment and of one's essential uselessness to others:

> De tout ce que j'ai dit de moi que reste-t-il
> J'ai conservé de faux trésors dans mes armoires vides
> Un navire inutile joint mon enfance à mon ennui (I, 412)[23]

> (Of all I have said of myself what remains
> I have kept false treasures in my empty cupboards
> A useless ship joins my childhood to my tedium).

The image of the useless ship is an echo of the "useless visage" Eluard describes himself as having had until the year 1918. But here the poet loses even the appearance of reality as his memories prove false and his language, empty. All the constructions undertaken and all the treasures contributed by the accomplishments of personal pride are negated by the rebirth of a vicious self-doubt.

And yet Eluard claims, in another poem from the same collection, that even the man "filled with emptiness" must continue to "seek the earth, " even though the journey is to be "A travers des rouilles mentales" (I, 444) / Across mental blights). The landscape is not all so melancholy:

> Le ciel éclatant joue dans le cirque vert
> . . .
> Le verre de la vallée est plein d'un feu limpide et doux.
>   (I, 443)

> (The blazing sky plays in the green hollow
> . . .
> The valley's glass is full of a fire gentle and limpid.)

The poet's vision is now of the future, of the "sure hours" of tomorrow and the day after. It is true that he is often able to call his poetry, as he does here, "Ce chant qui tient la nuit" (I, 429) / (This song containing the night), and that he sees it moving in the depths of "abolished roads"; but he is, toward the end of the poem, as sure as he was in his first poems of the poet's intimate and necessary relationship to the universe: "La lumière me soutient" (I, 444) / (The light sustains me).

Although these examples are simple, Eluard's alternations from one side of the contrary perceptions to the other are full of nuance, and they extend to all the facets of his poetry and his theory, complicating the simple surface.

For Eluard, as for all the surrealist poets, poetry is a clear but marvelous extension of vision and of comprehension, and an enlargement or crescendo of "reality." The deliberate expansion of poetic consciousness depends on a continuous series of contradictions, on the possibility of shifting from extreme to extreme, while the poet participates in all the movement and in all the vitality of which awareness is possible, reflecting and repeating the world and refusing

any interior limits: "Je ne veux pas finir en moi." He is the double
of the elements surrounding him, and their being enlarges his own:
"Et je respire et je me double / Du vent ... " (II, 428). Not only is
the individual consciousness identified with the consciousness of all
those around him, but now he is able to move high and low, near
and far, to feel himself vague and precise, "immense et plus petit";
in all directions, he is able to extend his apprehensions beyond the
normal state in which such oppositions would be impossible: This is
the perfect manifestion of what I am calling his multiconsciousness.

> Je suis la foule partout
> Des profondeurs et des hauteurs. (II 686)

> (I am the crowd everywhere
> Of the depths and of the heights.)

Of course, in the poems of war and of grief, it is just this *expansion* which is suddenly forbidden. Cracked or immobile mirrors
replace those Eluard usually associates with motion ("miroirs mou-
vants"), and the passionate identification with the multitude and the
exalted consciousness of multiplicity yield to a desperate solitude:

> La foule de mon corps en souffre
> Je m'affaiblis je me disperse. (I, 1126)

> (The crowd of my body suffers from it
> I am weakening I scatter.)

This is a poetry of reduction and absence, whose exact opposite
is the expansive poetry of surrealist vision. Eluard's most despair-
ing poems are haunted by the spectacle of walls closing in to shut
off liberty and light, and with them, the sense of man's individual
significance. He forgets and is forgotten by all, as his image, once
unique "à sa propre lumière," fades away, and light succumbs to
death:

Il n'y a de murs que pour moi

. . .

Entre les murs l'ombre est entière
Et je descends dans mon miroir
Comme un mort dans sa tombe ouverte. (I, 1021)

(Walls exist for me alone

. . .

Between the walls the shadow is complete
And I go down into my mirror
Like a dead man into his open tomb.)

Here a morbid self-consciousness takes precedence once more over the poet's lucid vision and ideal expansiveness ("Hors de nous-mêmes"); the poem is entitled "Mourir." A parallel poem, ironically entitled "Jouer," ends with the poet's realization that he no longer has a reflection at all. Eluard, again like Aragon and the early Breton, is always preoccupied by his own image and its preservation, both in his own mind and in the sight of others. This explains his fascination with mirrors and eyes, and his dread of walls and shadows which contradict light and are the absolute denial of reflection and of potential multiplicity. The preceding quotation is from his wartime poems, where the sensation of darkness and separation are to be expected; but walls and shadows haunt all his poetry, accompanied by various deformations of vision and reflection.[24] The "visible poems" called *A l'intérieur de la vue* (1948) present a further and less obvious problem: in spite of the multitude of ideas and projects envisioned by the complexity of the poet's "yeux variés," in spite of his overwhelming desire to change everything, the human limits of perception impose a dull and perpetual symmetry. All reflections and all responses are gradually reduced to a "mouvement banal," and even the infinite multiplicity of a poetic imagination cannot resist a daily exposure: "J'ai tout perdu dans ce miroir où l'on cuit le pain quotidien, où l'on reproduit dans l'ombre mes secrets, à l'infini." (II, 156) / (I have lost everything in this mirror where the daily bread is baked, where my secrets are reproduced in the shade, infinitely.)

Eluard's love poems present exactly the opposite vision. In its striking innocence and essential purity, surrealist love is the human equivalent of the image, miraculous in its unfailing capability of restoring the poet to a perfect world of immediacy and presence. As the whole calendar of days is seen emerging from a single dawn, so a single kiss is infinitely reproduced with the "faith of eternal youth" by the woman, whose endless complexities and contradictions it reveals: "Inconstante conjuguée / Captive infidèle et folle." She is at once the rain and the good weather, she appears: "Avec les plus fiers présents / Et les plus lointains absents." Again according to the notion of "one within the other, " the woman loved is at once all women, and at the same time, unique: "Present a specific woman but not man or woman."[25] Eluard addresses in his *Capitale de la douleur* "celle de toujours, toute," whom he never ceases to celebrate:

> O toi qui supprimes l'oubli, l'espoir et l'ignorance,
> Qui supprimes l'absence et qui me mets au monde
> . . .
> Tu es pure, tu es encore plus pure que moi-même. (I, 197)

> (You who abolish forgetfulness, ignorance, and hope
> You who suppress absence and give me birth
> . . .
> You are pure, you are even purer than I.)

All Eluard's love poems to Gala, to Nusch, and to Dominique are infused with this sense of purity and presence. For the poet, the woman loved has a power sufficient to overcome all consciousness of distance, spatial ("l'absence") or temporal ("l'oubli"); she offers him a "perpetual childhood" of immediacy and fulfills all his "desires of light." His reliance on the individual woman is mirrored in his poetry. When Nusch dies, Eluard's poems are filled with images of black corridors and despair; when Dominique appears, the miraculous transformations, the luminous order, and the intertwining of dualities reappear in their extreme simplicity:"

> O toi mon agitée et ma calme pensée
> Mon silence sonore et mon écho secret
> Mon aveugle voyante et ma vue dépassée
> Je n'ai plus eu que ta présence (II, 424)

> (You my restless and my calm thought
> My resounding silence and my secret echo
> My blind clairvoyant and my vision exceeded
> Since then I have possessed nothing but your presence).

But the last step in shedding all traces of self-consciousness ("I am the woman") and in piercing "the wall of my mirror" has not been taken until the poet is able to love the woman precisely for her difference from him even while he is completely identified with her: "Connais ce qui n'est pas à ton image" / (Know what is not in your own image).

> Je t'aime pour ta sagesse qui n'est pas la mienne
> . . .
> Pour ce coeur immortel qui je ne détiens pas. (II, 439)

> (I love you for your wisdom that is not mine
> . . .
> For this immortal heart that I do not possess.)

For the principle of one within the other requires that neither the one nor the other be lost. The realization of the surrealist marvelous depends on the continually recreated unity of two separate things; if either is absorbed, the specifically dynamic quality of the marvelous is denied and only a staid and stable compound remains, ruling out any future possibility of interconnection.

The many forms of oppositions which surrealist poets unceasingly perceive within themselves and their relationships toward the exterior world are intensified and made concrete in their relations with the beloved. First of all, the woman celebrated in surrealist poetry is not simply an individual who is pictured in detail, but is at once herself and all women ("une pour toutes"). Her qualities and her actions are as general as they are specific, as Eluard pictures her for instance in the famous prose poem "Nuits partagées" from *La Vie immédiate,* where she takes off her dress "avec la plus grande simplicité."[26] She dreams of uniting the contraries by the force of her own conflicting qualities:

> Par ta force et par ta faiblesse, tu croyais pouvoir concilier
> les désaccords de la présence et les harmonies de l'absence

> (By your strength and by your weakness, you thought
> you could reconcile the disagreements of presence and the
> harmonies of absence),

and for a time she manages "une union maladroite, naïve." Yet underlying the perceptions of unity offered by both the spirit of the *merveilleux* and of the *naïf* is a sophisticated double, world-wearing and even image-wearing:

> Mais, plus bas que tout, il y avait l'ennui.

> (But deeper than everything there was tedium.)

Surrealist woman is full of "calm and freshness . . . of salt of water of sun" and at the same time, of a "violent youth disquiet and saturated with tedium. "Nuits partagées" is in its tone and setting remarkably appropriate to the double but ideally unifying nature of woman, "one or many" as she is seen by the surrealist poet, and to the alternating sentiments of surrealist love.

La lumière m'a pourtant donné de belles images des négatifs de nos rencontres. Je t'ai identifée à des êtres dont seule la variété justifiait le nom, toujours le même, le tien, dont je voulais les nommer, des êtres que je transformais comme je te transformais, en pleine lumière . . . .La neige même, qui fut derrière nous l'écran douloureux sur lequel les cristaux des serments fondaient, la neige même était masquée. Dans les cavernes terrestres, des plantes cristallisées cherchaient les décolletés de la sortie.

Ténèbres abyssales toutes tendues vers une confusion éblouissante, je ne m'apercevais pas que ton nom devenait illusoire.

(But the light has given me beautiful pictures of the negatives of our encounters. I identified you with beings whose variety alone justified the name that I wanted to call them by, always the same one, yours—beings whom I transformed as I transformed you, in total light . . . . The snow itself, which was the sorrowful screen behind us where the crystals of vows melted, the snow itself was masked. In the caves of earth, crystallized plants sought the deep fissures of the exit.

Abysmal darkness stretched toward a dazzling confusion, I did not notice that your name was becoming illusory.)

The play of light and shadow and the parallel balance of reality and illusion are both pathetic and subtle, as they gradually move from positive poetic transformations toward the disintegration of fidelity and certainty, where the melting crystals of human promises contrast with, and yet equal in their reverse progression, the plants unnaturally fixed into crystalline hardness. The development is as natural as the phenomenon of melting snow, and yet it can be read as an experiment in photographic trickery with its superpositions and metamorphoses, in which the poet claims and disclaims an active role. He deliberately multiplies and transforms the woman's image, but it is the light that provides him with the pictures of their union and it is the snow that provides the melancholy and ambiguous (masked) background for their vows. This is a perfect example of surrealist poetry in its sucessful combination of logic and illogic, obvious simplicity and implied complexity.

Love is the *irreducible* counterpart of poetry, as it suppresses all the distances included in ordinary sight and at the same time requires and favors an expansion temporal and spatial, metaphysical and actual, contradictory and unitary. As the unique woman is simultaneously many women, she reflects the image of the poet himself as a multitude of individuals, each participating entirely in the multiple and single truth to which she bears witness. Her eyes not only mirror his multiple reflection, but they give birth to an infinite series of reflections:

> Multiple tes yeux divers et confondus
> Font fleurir les miroirs. (I, 460)

> (Multiple your eyes diverse and mingled
> Make mirrors flower.)

> Ce miroir sans limites. (II, 58)

> (This limitless mirror.)

Whereas the poet has been unable alone to "pierce the wall" of his mirror, he is now extended and illuminated in a necessarily double and paradoxical relationship: "Rien n'est simple ni singulier." (II, 442) / (Nothing is simple or singular.) The concept of love as reflection is inextricably linked with the concept of multiplication: "Constant amour multiplé tout nu / Volume espace de l'amour / Multiplié"; "Tu multiplies mon cœur et mon corps et mes sens"; "Je t'appellerai Visuelle / Et multiplierai ton image"; "Entre en moi toi ma multitude / Puisque je suis à jamais ton miroir / Ma figurée." Even the reverse side of the multiple vision is exemplified in the love poems, where eternity has unfolded ("s'est dépliée"), so that what appeared closed has opened out into many parts.

But just as constant as the renewal of vision is the alternation of hope and despair, appropriate to the two elements of the relationship of love. Each of the partners is the double for the other, in a constant clarity of reflection, and yet that reflection itself has its own double, which denies it: "Je ne suis plus le miroir." Sentiments are not simple, they are at least dual. For a surrealist, human desire is unquestionably the supreme example of dynamic extension and unceasing motion:

> Désirs chemins mouvants (I, 833)

> (Désires moving paths)

and still the motion itself comes *inevitably* to a sudden halt:

> Mime gêlé l'amour est immobile (I, 837)

> (Love is motionless frozen pantomime).

Only the images on the surface of the poem remain in constant play. The theater of language continues to function when the human poet is the most conscious of his own weakness.

The experiences of clear vision, multiplication, metamorphosis, and extension are submitted to the terrible tests of darkness and invisibility, reduction and immobility. For even the ideal universe of "resemblances" itself has a double, and this double is the most tragic in its implications:

> Les resemblances ne sont pas en rapport,
> Elles se heurtent. (II, 221)

(Similarities do not relate,
They clash against each other.)

The surrealist poet establishes endless sets of relationships from distant elements, in the faith that this new poetic universe will hold up against the other. But the attempt to build a whole system on the power of analogies, on even the most passionate conviction in the existence of a supremely strong *fil conducteur*, is a risky one. The force of juxtapositions and marvelous perceptions is not always easy to transfer outside the realm of the poem: Lautréamont, after all, did not try to construct a whole system on the encounter of the umbrella and the sewing machine. It is marvelous that they should meet on a dissection table—but momentary examples of *le merveilleux* do not forever guarantee either the permanence of vision or the duration of the miracle.

Eluard is in some senses a simple poet, and certainly he is a poet of a simple, luminous love in all its purity and its order: "Beaux yeux *ordonnez* la lumière"; "Et des jours et des nuits *réglés* par tes paupières"; "Et je me suis trouvé *réglé* comme un aimant / *Réglé* comme une vigne"; "Le feu *mit en ordre* la fête."[27] But more significantly, he is a surrealist poet, faithful until the end of his life to the play of dualities which give to surrealism its genuine profundity and its unlimited potentiality of expansion. In the volume of Eluard's last love poems, there are brief and therefore often overlooked references to the essential alternation scattered among his famous images of pure radiance, The *vision* is not simple; it includes both the opaque and the transparent, the fresh and the aging:

De la boue et de la rosée. (II, 421)

(Mud and dew.)

———

La rosée et la rouille. (II, 686)

(The dew and the rust.)

Eluard takes as much pride in his experiences of the "ravines" as those of the summits; the profundity of his feeling and of his expression comes exactly from the awareness of contraries, so that he can say, in these last poems: "Et nous voici plus bas et plus haut que jamais." (II, 421) / (And now we are lower and higher than ever.)

Deprived of the darker images, the rage of surrealist perspective would be far more limited, incapable of the tension stretching between extremes on which its peculiar strength depends. The consciousness of possible height is magnified and extended by the opposite consciousness, its necessary counterpart in this typically surrealist vision of love.

Capital of Pain is, as the title indicates, full of anguish. Personal anguish. In 1924, exhausted emotionally by the quite extraordinary *ménage à trois* with the high-strung and willfully erotic Gala and the immensely attractive Max Ernst—gaunt, with his eagle face and features—Eluard fled France for six months. He returned finally, but traces of his anguish remain for all to read in the book he was to publish two years later, a document of pain, sometimes transformed into precious, playful, or light-tempered poems, sometimes distilled as pure violence, as in the two poems at the center of the collection, both named "In the Flame of the Lash." Each white-hot line of this crucial double poem renders as concrete imagery the poet's suffering and the multiconsciousness of the text quoted above, "Je suis la femme et son mari et leur enfant," with its devastating final lines:

> And even when a body is undone in death
> I lie in its crucible I wed its torment.

The poet's searing ability to lie in the crucible of the other, to embrace the pain he encounters there, in death as in love, is articulated anew with every stroke of the lash, his own torment inescapable, echoing throughout his *Capital of Pain*.

NOTES:

1   Karl Marx, quoted in Paul Eluard, *Anthologie des écrits sur l'art* (Editions Cercle d'art, 1952), p. 93.
2   *ibid., p. 97.*
3   *La Poésie du passé* (Seghers, 1951), p. 14.
4   "Baigneuse du clair au sombre," *Les Nécessités de la vie, poèmes* (Gallimard, 1951), p. 46.
5   Essay of 1934, printed in *Beyond Painting* (New York, Wittenborn, 1948).
6   *Avenir de la poésie* (G.L.M., 1937).
7   *A Pablo Picasso* (Geneva, Editions Trois Collines, 1944), p 31.
8   "Aujourd'hui," *Poèmes politiques* (Gallimard, 1948).
9   *Poésie ininterrompue*, II (Gallimard, 1953), p. 36.
10 Quoted in *L'Art poétique*, J. Charpier, ed. (Seghers, 1952), p. 664.
11 *Anthologie des écrits sur l'art*, p.8
12 "Préliminaires sur Matta," *Le Surréalisme et la peinture* (Gallimard, 1966).
13 Essay of 1934, printed in *Beyond Painting* (New York, Wittenborn, 1948).
14 "Mes heures," *Le Livre ouvert*. Il La Nécessité, " *La Vie immédiate*. Compare Tzara's: « Comprendre, voir. »
15 "D'un et deux, de tous," *Les Derniers poèmes d'amour* (Seghers, 1966).
16 Compare with Desnos' poem "le Paysage," where again the poet is in some sense a prisoner of his own landscape. Eluard's poem is addressed "à celle qui répète ce que je dis"—thus the feminine form. Note also the theme of repetition and reflection.
17 In fact, Eluard deliberately chooses a simple form so as not to place a barrier between himself and any reader; the poem should be equivalent to the song—instantly comprehensible. (See Eluard's note on poetry as song [II, 931], and chapter 2, note 12.)
18 « Quelques uns des mots qui, jusqu'ici, m'étaient mystérieusement interdits. »
19 Compare with this poem the similar poem "A la fin de l'Année: de jour en jour plus bas, il enfouit sa chaleur comme une graine," in the 1936 volume *Facile*, which also exemplifies the vision described in Eluard's speech of 1937, *L'avenir de la poésie*, of a "reciprocal" poetry, based on equal happiness for all. Both poems are based on the themes of approach, of unique intensity, baraeness and brilliance, equivalence and fraternity, and they share the same rhythms and the same imagery:

> Nous avançons toujours
> . . .
> Nous vivons d'un seul jet
> Nous sommes du bon port
> . . .
> Nos baisers et nos mains au niveau de nous-mêmes
> La jeunesse en amande se dénude et rêve
> L'herbe se relève en sourdine
> . . .
> Toute brume chassée

. . .
Notre ombre n'éteint pas le feu
Nous nous perpétuons.

(We always go forward
. . .
We live all at once
We are assured

. . .
Our kisses and our hands at our own level
Youth like an almond disrobes and dreams
The grass rises in secret

. . .
All mist dispersed

. . .
Our shadow does not put out the fire
We perpetuate ourselves.)

20 *Jacques Villon ou l'art glorieux* (Louis Carré, 1948), p. 32.
21 "Ah!," *Pour vivre ici,* repeated in *Les Nécessités de la vie et les conséquences des rêves* (Au Sans Pareil, 1921).
22 "Salon," *Les Animaux et leurs hommes* (Au Sans Pareil, 1920).
23 A terrible contrast to Breton's "enchantment" with his own despair in "Le Verbe être" of two years earlier.
24 The mirror is seen as a wall when it only sends back the single reflection. That is, before the reflection is doubled by the interrelations of personalities and presences, its connotation of sterility and vacancy is inescapable. But it also signifies a certain distance from the interior spectacle, as does the window from the exterior spectacle (see Chapter 2): "But the really clever person is the one who has managed to see his eye without the aid of a glass, the one who has let his gaze wander over the voluptuous hollow in the back of his neck. Ah, may the day come when we can break the mirror, that final window, when our eyes can at last contemplate the *cerebral marvelous.*" *Les Feuilles libres* (January–February 1924).
25 "Physique de la poésie," *Minotaure, 6.*
26 And yet even this simplicity can imply its contrary: "Elle est . . . d'une grande simplicité artificielle" (I, 379)
27 Emphasis added.

Mary Ann Caws is Distinguished Professor of English, French, and Comparative Literature at the Graduate School of The City University of New York. She is the author, translator, and editor of numerous books and publications on the major figures of both Dada and Surrealism. Recent books by Professor Caws include: *Henry James* (*Illustrated Lives*) and *Surprised in Translation*. Forthcoming books include: *Glorious Eccentrics: Modernist Women Painting and Writing*, *The Essential Poems and Writing of Robert Desnos*, and with Patricia Terry, a revised edition of *Roof Slates and Other Poems of Pierre Reverdy*.

Patricia Terry was Professor of French Literature at Barnard College and the University of California San Diego until her retirement in 1991. Among her verse translations are *Poems of Jules Laforgue*, *The Song of Roland*, *Poems of the Elder Edda*, *The Honeysuckle and the Hazel Tree*, *Renard the Fox*, and *Roof Slates and Other Poems of Pierre Reverdy* (with Mary Ann Caws). At present she is working on a new edition of Laforgue and an anthology of poems by Guillevic. A book of her own poems, *Words of Silence*, was published by Higganum Hill Press in 2005.

Nancy Kline directs the Writing Program at Barnard College, where she teaches in the English and the French Departments. She has published five books to date, including: *The Faithful* (a novel), *Lightning: The Poetry of René Char*, and *Elizabeth Blackwell, MD: A Doctor's Triumph* (a biography). She is currently working on a novel entitled *Strings* and an essay collection entitled *Other Geographies*. Her numerous translations, essays, short stories, and reviews have appeared widely.

All Black Widow Press titles are printed on acid-free paper and bound into a sewn and glued binding. Manufactured in the United States of America.

www.blackwidowpress.com

This book was set in Adobe's Cronos Pro, designed by Robert Slimbach as a modern sans serifed type based on oldstyle roman letterforms, and ITC's Stone Serif, designed by John Renner as a modern typeface based on Transitional type styles. The titling font is Aculida, a modernistic typeface used by many of the Dadaists in their typographic artworks.

typeset & designed by Windhaven Press
www.windhaven.com

green press
INITIATIVE

Black Widow Press is committed to preserving ancient forests and natural resources. We elected to print *Capital Of Pain* on 50% post consumer recycled paper, processed chlorine free. As a result, for this printing, we have saved:

14 Trees (40' tall and 6-8" diameter)
5,862 Gallons of Waste Water
2,358 Kilowatt Hours of Electricity
644 Pounds of Solid Waste
1,269 Pounds of Greenhouse Gases

Black Widow Press made this paper choice because our printer, Thomson-Shore, Inc., is a member of Green Press Initiative, a nonprofit program dedicated to supporting authors, publishers, and suppliers in their efforts to reduce their use of fiber obtained from endangered forests.

For more information, visit www.greenpressinitiative.org

TITLES FROM BLACK WIDOW PRESS

TRANSLATION SERIES

A Life of Poems, Poems of a Life
by Anna de Noailles. Translated by Norman
R. Shapiro. Introduction by Catherine Perry.

Approximate Man and Other Writings
by Tristan Tzara. Translated and edited
by Mary Ann Caws.

Art Poétique
by Guillevic. Translated by Maureen Smith.

The Big Game
by Benjamin Péret. Translated with an
introduction by Marilyn Kallet.

Capital of Pain
by Paul Eluard. Translated by Mary Ann
Caws, Patricia Terry, and Nancy Kline.

Chanson Dada: Selected Poems
by Tristan Tzara. Translated with an
introduction and essay by Lee Harwood.

*Essential Poems and Writings of Joyce Mansour:
A Bilingual Anthology*
Translated with an introduction by
Serge Gavronsky.

Essential Poems and Prose of Jules Laforgue
Translated and edited by Patricia Terry.

*Essential Poems and Writings of Robert Desnos:
A Bilingual Anthology*
Edited with an introduction and essay by
Mary Ann Caws.

EyeSeas (Les Ziaux)
by Raymond Queneau. Translated with an
introduction by Daniela Hurezanu and
Stephen Kessler.

Furor and Mystery & Other Writings
by René Char. Edited and translated by
Mary Ann Caws and Nancy Kline.

The Inventor of Love & Other Writings
by Gherasim Luca. Translated by Julian
and Laura Semilian. Introduction by
Andrei Codrescu. Essay by Petre Răileanu.

La Fontaine's Bawdy
by Jean de La Fontaine. Translated with
an introduction by Norman R. Shapiro.

Last Love Poems of Paul Eluard
Translated with an introduction by
Marilyn Kallet.

Love, Poetry (L'amour la poésie)
by Paul Eluard. Translated with an essay
by Stuart Kendall.

Poems of André Breton: A Bilingual Anthology
Translated with essays by Jean-Pierre
Cauvin and Mary Ann Caws.

Poems of A.O. Barnabooth
by Valéry Larbaud. Translated by Ron Padgett
and Bill Zavatsky.

Préversities: A Jacques Prévert Sampler
Translated and edited by Norman R. Shapiro.

The Sea and Other Poems
by Guillevic. Translated by Patricia Terry.
Introduction by Monique Chefdor.

To Speak, to Tell You? Poems by Sabine Sicaud.
Translated by Norman R. Shapiro. Introduction and notes by Odile Ayral-Clause.

forthcoming translations

Jules Choppin (1830–1914)
New Orleans Poems in Creole and French.
Translated by Norman R. Shapiro.

Poems of Consummation
by Vicente Aleixandre. Translated by
Stephen Kessler

MODERN POETRY SERIES

An Alchemist with One Eye on Fire
by Clayton Eshleman

Anticline by Clayton Eshleman

Archaic Design by Clayton Eshleman

Backscatter: New and Selected Poems
by John Olson

The Caveat Onus by Dave Brinks
The complete cycle, four volumes in one.

City Without People: The Katrina Poems
by Niyi Osundare

Concealments and Caprichos
by Jerome Rothenberg

Crusader-Woman
by Ruxandra Cesereanu. Translated by Adam
J. Sorkin. Introduction by Andrei Codrescu.

Curdled Skulls: Poems of Bernard Bador
Translated by the author with
Clayton Eshleman.

Endure: Poems
by Bei Dao. Translated by Clayton Eshleman
and Lucas Klein.

Exile is My Trade: A Habib Tengour Reader
Translated by Pierre Joris.

Fire Exit by Robert Kelly

Forgiven Submarine
by Ruxandra Cesereanu and Andrei Codrescu

from stone this running by Heller Levinson

The Grindstone of Rapport:
A Clayton Eshleman Reader
Forty years of poetry, prose, and translations.

Larynx Galaxy by John Olson

Memory Wing by Bill Lavender

Packing Light: New and Selected Poems
by Marilyn Kallet

The Present Tense of the World:
Poems 2000–2009 by Amina Saïd. Translated
with an introduction by Marilyn Hacker.

Signal from Draco: New and Selected Poems
by Mebane Robertson

forthcoming modern poetry titles

ABC of Translation by Willis Barnstone

An American Unconscious
by Mebane Robertson

Eye of Witness: A Jerome Rothenberg Reader
Edited with commentaries by Heriberto
Yepez & Jerome Rothenberg

Memory by Bernadette Mayer

My Secret Brain: Selected Poems
by Dave Brinks

The Price of Experience by Clayton Eshleman

LITERARY THEORY / BIOGRAPHY SERIES

Revolution of the Mind:
The Life of André Breton by Mark Polizzotti.
Revised and augmented edition.

WWW.BLACKWIDOWPRESS.COM